The Two Noble Kinsmen
by John Fletcher & William Shakespeare

John Fletcher was born in December, 1579 in Rye, Sussex. He was baptised on December 20th.

As can be imagined details of much of his life and career have not survived and, accordingly, only a very brief indication of his life and works can be given.

Young Fletcher appears at the very young age of eleven to have entered Corpus Christi College at Cambridge University in 1591. There are no records that he ever took a degree but there is some small evidence that he was being prepared for a career in the church.

However what is clear is that this was soon abandoned as he joined the stream of people who would leave University and decamp to the more bohemian life of commercial theatre in London.

The upbringing of the now teenage Fletcher and his seven siblings now passed to his paternal uncle, the poet and minor official Giles Fletcher. Giles, who had the patronage of the Earl of Essex may have been a liability rather than an advantage to the young Fletcher. With Essex involved in the failed rebellion against Elizabeth Giles was also tainted.

By 1606 John Fletcher appears to have equipped himself with the talents to become a playwright. Initially this appears to have been for the Children of the Queen's Revels, then performing at the Blackfriars Theatre.

Fletcher's early career was marked by one significant failure; The Faithful Shepherdess, his adaptation of Giovanni Battista Guarini's Il Pastor Fido, which was performed by the Blackfriars Children in 1608.

By 1609, however, he had found his stride. With his collaborator John Beaumont, he wrote Philaster, which became a hit for the King's Men and began a profitable association between Fletcher and that company. Philaster appears also to have begun a trend for tragicomedy.

By the middle of the 1610s, Fletcher's plays had achieved a popularity that rivalled Shakespeare's and cemented the pre-eminence of the King's Men in Jacobean London. After his frequent early collaborator John Beaumont's early death in 1616, Fletcher continued working, both singly and in collaboration, until his own death in 1625. By that time, he had produced, or had been credited with, close to fifty plays.

William Shakespeare was born in Stratford-upon-Avon in late April 1565 and baptised there on 26th April. He was one of eight children.

Little is known about his life but what is evident is the enormous contribution he has made to world literature.

His writing was progressive, magnificent in scope and breathtaking in execution.

Shakespeare's plays and sonnets helped enable the English language to speak with a voice unmatched by any other.

William Shakespeare died on April 23rd 1616, survived by his wife and two daughters. He was buried two days after his death in the chancel of the Holy Trinity Church. The epitaph on the slab which covers his grave includes the following passage,

Good friend, for Jesus's sake forbear,
To dig the dust enclosed here.
Blessed me the man that spares these stones,
And cursed be he that moves my bones.

Index of Contents

DRAMATIS PERSONAE

Hymen,
Theseus,
Hippolita   }
Emelia   } Sisters to Theseus
Nymphs,
Three Queens,
Three valiant Knights,
Palamon   } The two Noble Kinsmen, in
Arcite   } love with fair Emelia.
Perithous,
Jaylor,
His Daughter, in love with Palamon,
Countrey-men,
Wenches,
A Taborer,
Gerrold, A Schoolmaster.

PROLOGUE

Flourish.

New Plays and Maiden-heads are near a-kin,
Much follow'd both; for both much money gi'n,
If they stand sound, and well: And a good Play
(Whose modest Scenes blush on his marriage day,
And shake to loose his honour) is like hir
That after holy Tie, and first nights stir
Yet still is Modesty, and still retains
More of the Maid to sight, than Husbands pains;
We pray our Play may be so; for I'm sure
It has a noble breeder, and a pure,
A Learned, and a Poet never went
More famous yet 'twixt Po, and silver Trent.
Chaucer (of all admir'd) the Story gives,
There constant to eternity it lives:
If we let fall the Nobleness of this,

And the first sound this Child hear, be a hiss,
How will it shake the bones of that good man
And make him cry from under-ground. Oh fan
From me the witless chaff of such a writer
That blasts my Bayes, and my fam'd Works makes lighter
Than Robin Hood, this is the fear we bring
For to say Truth, it were an endless thing:
And too ambitious to aspire to him;
Weak as we are, and almost breathless swim
In this deep water. Do but you hold out
Your helping hands, and we shall tack about,
And something do to save us: You shall hear
Scænes, though below his Art, may yet appear
Worth two hours travel. To his bones sweet sleep:
Content to you. If this Play do not keep,
A little dull time from us, we perceive
Our losses fall so thick, we must needs leave.

Flourish.

ACTUS PRIMUS

SCÆNA PRIMA

Enter **HYMEN** with a Torch burning: a **BOY**, in a white Robe before, singing, and strewing Flowers: after **HYMEN**, a **NYMPH**, encompassed in her Tresses, bearing a wheaten Garland. Then **THESEUS** between two other **NYMPHS**, with wheaten Chaplets on their heads. Then **HIPPOLITA** the Bride lead by **THESEUS**, and another holding a Garland over her head (her Tresses likewise hanging.) After her **EMILIA** holding up her Train.

[The SONG.

[Musick.

Roses their sharp spines being gone,
Not royal in their smells alone,
But in their hew,
Maiden-Pinks, of odour faint,
Daizies smell-less, yet most quaint
And sweet Time true.

Primrose first born, child of Ver,
Merry Spring time's Harbinger,
With her bels dimm.
Oxlips in their Cradles growing,
Marigolds on death-beds blowing,

Larks-heels trim.
All dear natures children sweet,
Lie fore Bride and Bridegrooms feet,

[Strew Flowers.

Blessing their sence.
Not an Angel of the Air,
Bird melodious, or Bird fair,
Is absent hence.

The Crow, the slanderous Cuckooe, nor
The boading Raven, nor Clough hee
Nor chatt'ring Pie,
May on our Bridehouse pearch or sing,
Or with them any discord bring
But from it fly.

[Enter three **QUEENS** in Black, with vails stain'd, with Imperial Crowns. The first **QUEEN** falls down at the foot of **THESEUS**; The **SECOND** fals down at the foot of **HIPPOLITA**. The **THIRD** before **EMILIA**.

1ST QUEEN
For pities sake, and true gentilities,
Hear and respect me.

2ND QUEEN
For your Mothers sake.
And as you wish your womb may thrive with fair ones,
Hear and respect me.

3RD QUEEN
Now for the love of him whom Jove hath mark'd
The honor of your Bed, and for the sake
Of clear Virginity, be Advocate
For us, and our distresses: This good deed
Shall raze you out o'th' Book of Trespasses
All you are set down there.

THESEUS
Sad Lady rise.

HIPPOLITO
Stand up.

EMILIA
No knees to me.
What Woman I may steed that is distrest,
Does bind me to her.

THESEUS
What's your request? Deliver you for all?

1ˢᵀ QUEEN
We are three Queens, whose Sovereigns fell before
The wrath of cruel Creon; who endur'd
The Beaks of Ravens, Tallents of the Kites,
And pecks of Crows in the foul fields of Thebs.
He will not suffer us to burn their bones,
To urne their ashes, nor to take th' offence
Of mortal loathsomness from the blest eye
Of holy Phoebus, but infects the winds
With stench of our slain Lords. Oh pity Duke,
Thou purger of the earth, draw thy fear'd Sword
That does good turns to th' world; give us the Bones
Of our dead Kings, that we may Chappel them;
And of thy boundless goodness take some note
That for our crowned heads we have no roof;
Save this which is the Lions and the Bears,
And vault to every thing.

THESEUS
Pray you kneel not,
I was transported with your Speech, and suffer'd
Your knees to wrong themselves; I have heard the fortunes
Of your dead Lords, which gives me such lamenting
As wakes my vengeance, and revenge for 'em:
King Capaneus, was your Lord the day
That he should marry you, at such a season,
As now it is with me, I met your Groom,
By Mars's Altar; you were that time fair;
Not Juno's Mantle, fairer than your Tresses,
Nor in more bounty spread her. Your wheaten wreath
Was then not thrash'd, nor blasted; Fortune at you
Dimpled her Cheek with smiles: Hercules our kinsman
(Then weaker than your eyes) laid by his Club,
He tumbled down upon his Nenuan hide
And swore his sinews thaw'd: Oh grief, and time,
Fearful consumers, you will all devour.

1ˢᵀ QUEEN
Oh I hope some God,
Some God hath put his mercy in your manhood
Whereto he'll infuse power, and press you forth
Our undertaker.

THESEUS

Oh no knees, none Widow,
Unto the Helmeted-Belona use them,
And pray for me your Soldier.
Troubl'd I am.

[Turns away.

2ᴺᴰ QUEEN

Honoured Hippolita
Most dreaded Amazonian, that hast slain
The Sith-tusk'd-Bore; that with thy Arm as strong
As it is white, was't near to make the male
To thy Sex captive; but that this thy Lord
Born to uphold Creation, in that honor
First nature stil'd it in, shrunk thee into
The bound thou wast o'er-flowing; at once subduing
Thy force, and thy affection: Soldieress
That equally canst poize sternness with pity,
Whom now I know hast much more power on him
Than ever he had on thee, who ow'st his strength,
And his Love too: who is a Servant for
The Tenor of the Speech. Dear Glass of Ladies.
Bid him that we whom flaming war doth scorch,
Under the shadow of his Sword, may cool us:
Require him he advance it o'er our heads;
Speak't in a womans key: like such a woman
As any of us three; weep e'r you fail; lend us a knee;
But touch the ground for us no longer time
Than a Doves motion, when the head's pluckt off:
Tell him if he i'th' blood-ciz'd field, lay swoln
Shewing the Sun his Teeth, grinning at the Moon
What you would do.

HIPPOLITO

Poor Lady say no more:
I had as leif trace this good action with you
As that whereto I'm going, and never yet
Went I so willing, way. My Lord is taken
Heart deep with your distress: Let him consider;
I'll speak anon.

3ᴿᴰ QUEEN

Oh my petition was,

[Kneel to **EMILIA**.

Set down in Ice, which by hot grief uncandied
Melts into drops, so sorrow wanting form

Is prest with deeper matter.

EMILIA
Pray stand up,
Your grief is written in your cheek.

3RD QUEEN

Oh woe,
You cannot read it there; there through my tears,
Like wrinkl'd pebbles in a Glass stream
You may behold 'em (Lady, Lady, alack)
He that will all the treasure know o'th' earth
Must know the Center too; he that will fish
For my least minnow, let him lead his line
To catch one at my heart. Oh pardon me;
Extremity that sharpens sundry wits
Makes me a fool.

EMILIA
Pray you say nothing, pray you,
Who cannot feel, nor see the rain being in't,
Knows neither wet, nor dry, if that you were
The ground-piece of some Painter, I would buy you
T'instruct me 'gainst a capital grief indeed
Such heart-pierc'd demonstration; but alas
Being a natural Sister of our Sex
Your sorrow beats so ardently upon me:
That it shall make a counter-reflect 'gainst
My Brothers heart, and warm it to some pity
Though it were made of stone: pray have good comfort:

THESEUS
Forward to th' Temple, leave not out a jot
O' th' sacred ceremony.

1ST QUEEN
Oh this celebration
Will long last, and be more costly than
Your Suppliants war: Remember that your Fame
Knowls in the ear o'th' world: what you do quickly,
Is not done rashly; your first thought is more,
Than others laboured meditance: your premeditating
More than their actions: But oh Jove, your actions,
Soon as they move, as Asprays do the fish,
Subdue before they touch: think, dear Duke think
What beds our slain Kings have.

2ND QUEEN

ALL QUEENS
Oh help now
Our Cause cries for your knee.

EMILIA
If you grant not
My Sister her petition in that force,
With that Celerity, and nature which
She makes it in: from henceforth I'll not dare
To ask you any thing, nor be so hardy
Ever to take a Husband.

THESEUS
Pray stand up.
I am intreating of my self to do
That which you kneel to have me; Pyrithous
Lead on the Bride; get you and pray the gods
For success, and return; omit not any thing
In the pretended Celebration; Queens
Follow your Soldier (as before) hence you
And at the banks of Anly meet us with
The forces you can raise, where we shall find
The moiety of a number, for a business,
More bigger look't; since that our Theme is haste
I stamp this kiss uppon thy currant Lip,
Sweet keep it as my token; set you forward
For I will see you gone.

[Exeunt towards the Temple.

Farewel my beauteous Sister; Perithous
Keep the Feast full, bate not an hour on't.

PERITHOUS
Sir,
I'll follow you at heels; The Feasts solemnity
Shall want till your return.

THESEUS
Cosin I charge you
Budge not from Athens; we shall be returning
E'r you can end this Feast; of which I pray you
Make no abatement; once more farewel all.

1ST QUEEN
Thus dost thou still make good the tongue o'th' world.

2ND QUEEN
And earnst a Deity equal with Mars.

3RD QUEEN
If not above him, for
Thou being but mortal, makest affections bend
To godlike honors; they themselves some say
Groan under such a Mast'ry.

THESEUS
As we are men
Thus should we doe, being sensually subdu'd
We loose our humane Title; good cheer Ladies.

[Flourish.

Now turn we towards our Comforts.

[Exeunt.

SCÆNA SECUNDA

Enter **PALAMON** and **ARCITE**.

ARCITE
Dear Palamon, dearer in Love than Blood
And our prime Cosin, yet unhard'ned in
The Crimes of nature; Let us leave the City
Thebs, and the temptings in't, before we further
Sully our gloss of youth,
And here to keep in abstinence we shame
As in Incontinence; for not to swim
I' th' aid o'th' current, were almost to sink,
At least to frustrate striving, and to follow
The common stream, 't would bring us to an Eddy
Where we should turn or drown; if labour through,
Our gain but life, and weakness.

PALAMON
Your advice
Is cry'd up with example; what strange ruins
Since first we went to School, may we perceive
Walking in Thebs! Skars, and bare weeds
The gain o'th' Martialist, who did propound
To his bold ends, honor, and golden Ingots,
Which though he won, he had not, and now flurted

By peace, for whom he fought, who then shall offer
To Mars's so scorn'd Altar? I doe bleed
When such I meet, and wish great Juno would
Resume her antient fit of jealousie
To get the Soldier work, that peace might purge
For her repletion, and retain anew
Her charitable heart now hard, and harsher
Than strife, or war could be.

ARCITE
Are you not out?
Meet you no ruin, but the Soldier in
The crancks and turns of Thebs? you did begin
As if you met decaies of many kinds:
Perceive you none, that do arouse your pity
But th' unconsider'd Soldier?

PALAMON
Yes, I pity
Decaies where-e'er I find them, but such most
That sweating in an honourable toil
Are paid with Ice to cool 'em.

ARCITE
'Tis not this
I did begin to speak of, this is virtue
Of no respect in Thebs, I spake of Thebs
How dangerous if we will keep our honors,
It is for our residing, where every evil
Hath a good colour; where ev'ry seeming good's
A certain evil, where not to be ev'n jump
As they are, here were to be strangers, and
Such things to be meer Monsters.

PALAMON
'Tis in our power,
(Unless we fear that Apes can Tutor's) to
Be Masters of our manners: what need I
Affect anothers gate, which is not catching
Where there is faith, or to be fond upon
Anothers way of speech, when by mine own
I may be reasonably conceiv'd; sav'd too,
Speaking it truly; why am I bound
By any generous bond to follow him
Follows his Taylor, haply so long, until
The follow'd, make pursuit? or let me know,
Why mine own Barber is unblest, with him
My poor Chinn too, for 'tis not Cizard just

To such a Favorites glass: What Cannon is there
That does command my Rapier from my hip
To dangle't in my hand, or to goe tip toe
Before the street be foul? either I am
The fore-horse in the Team, or I am none
That draw i' th' sequent trace: these poor slight sores,
Need not a Plantain; That which rips my bosome
Almost to th' heart's.

ARCITE
Our Uncle Creon.

PALAMON
He,
A most unbounded Tyrant, whose successes
Makes Heaven unfear'd, and villany assured
Beyond its power: there's nothing, almost puts
Faith in a Feavor, and deifies alone
Voluble chance, who only attributes
The faculties of other Instruments
To his own Nerves and act; Commands men service,
And what they win in't, boot and glory on;
That fears not to do harm; good, dares not; Let
The bloud of mine that's sibbe to him, be suckt
From me with Leeches, let them break and fall
Off me with that corruption.

ARCITE
Clear spirited Cosin
Let's leave his Court, that we may nothing share,
Of his loud infamy: for our milk,
Will relish of the pasture, and we must
Be vile, or disobedient, not his kinsmen
In blood, unless in quality.

PALAMON
Nothing truer:
I think the ecchoes of his shames have deaf't
The ears of heav'nly Justice: widdows cries
Descend again into their throats, and have not
Due audience of the gods: Valerius.

[Enter **VALERIUS**.

VALERIUS
The King calls for you; yet be leaden-footed
Till his great rage be off him. Phebus when
He broke his whipstock, and exclaim'd against

The Horses of the Sun, but whisper'd to
The loudness of his fury.

PALAMON
Small winds shake him,
But what's the matter?

VALERIUS
Theseus (who where he threats appals,) hath sent
Deadly defiance to him, and pronounces
Ruin to Thebs, who is at hand to seal
The promise of his wrath.

ARCITE
Let him approach:
But that we fear the gods in him, he brings not
A jot of terror to us; yet what man
Thirds his own worth (the case is each of ours)
When that his actions dregg'd, with mind assur'd
'Tis bad he goes about.

PALAMON
Leave that unreason'd.
Our services stand now for Thebs, not Creon,
Yet to be neutral to him, were dishonor;
Rebellious to oppose: therefore we must
With him stand to the mercy of our Fate,
Who hath bounded our last minute.

ARCITE
So we must;
Ist sed this wars afoot? or it shall be
On fail of some condition.

VALERIUS
'Tis in motion
The intelligence of state came in the instant
With the defier.

PALAMON
Let's to the King, who, were he
A quarter carrier of that honor, which
His enemy came in, the bloud we venture
Should be as for our health, which were not spent,
Rather laid out for purchase: but alas
Our hands advanc'd before our hearts, what will
The fall o' th' stroke do damage?

ARCITE
Let th' event,
That never-erring Arbitrator, tell us
When we know all our selves, and let us follow
The becking of our chance.

[Exeunt.

SCÆNA TERTIA

Enter **PERITHOUS, HIPPOLITA, EMILIA**.

PERITHOUS
No further.

HIPPOLITO
Sir farewel; repeat my wishes
To our great Lord, of whose success I dare not
Make any timerous question; yet I wish him
Excess, and overflow of power, and't might be
To dure ill-dealing fortune; speed to him,
Store never hurts good Governors.

PERITHOUS
Though I know
His Ocean needs not my poor drops, yet they
Must yield their tribute there: My precious Maid,
Those best affections that the heavens infuse
In their best temper'd pieces, keep enthron'd
In your dear heart.

EMILIA
Thanks Sir; remember me
To our all-Royal Brother, for whose speed
The great Bellona I'll solicite; and
Since in our terrene State, petitions are not
Without gifts understood: I'll offer to her
What I shall be advis'd she likes; our hearts
Are in his Army, in his Tent.

HIPPOLITO
In's bosom:
We have been Soldiers, and we cannot weep
When our Friends do'n their helms, or put to Sea,
Or tell of Babes broach'd on the Launce, or Women
That have sod their Infants in (and after eat them)

The brine, they wept at killing 'em; Then if
You stay to see of us such Spinsters, we
Should hold you here for ever.

PERITHOUS
Peace be to you
As I pursue this war, which shall be then
Beyond further requiring.

[Exit **PERITHOUS**.

EMILIA
How his longing
Follows his friend; since his depart, his sports
Though craving seriousness, and skill, past slightly
His careless execution, where nor gain
Made him regard, or loss consider, but
Playing o'er business in his hand, another
Directing in his head, his mind, nurse equal
To these so diff'ring Twins; have you observ'd him,
Since our great Lord departed?

HIPPOLITO
With much labour:
And I did love him for't, they two have Cabin'd
In many as dangerous, as poor a corner,
Peril and want contending, they have skift
Torrents, whose roaring tyranny and power
I'th' least of these was dreadful, and they have
Fought out together, where Death's-self was lodg'd,
Yet Fate hath brought them off: their knot of love
Ti'd, weav'd, intangl'd, with so true, so long,
And with a finger of so deep a cunning
May be out-worn, never undone. I think
Theseus cannot be umpire to himself
Cleaving his conscience into twain, and doing
Each side like Justice, which he loves best.

EMILIA
Doubtless
There is a best, and reason has no manners
To say it is not you: I was acquainted
Once with a time, when I enjoy'd a Play-fellow;
You were at wars, when she the grave enrich'd,
Who made too proud the Bed, took leave o' th' Moon
(Which then lookt pale at parting) when our count
Was each eleven.

HIPPOLITO
'Twas Flavia.

[Two Hearses ready with **PALAMON** and **ARCITE**: The **THREE QUEENS**. **THESEUS**, and his **LORDS** ready.

EMILIA
Yes,
You talk of Pirithous and Theseus love;
Theirs has more ground, is more maturely season'd,
More buckled with strong judgement, and their needs
The one of th' other may be said to water
Their intertangled roots of love, but I
And she (I sigh and spoke of) were things innocent,
Lov'd for we did, and like the Elements
That know not what, nor why, yet do effect
Rare issues by their operance; our souls
Did so to one another; what she lik'd,
Was then of me approv'd, what not condemn'd
No more arraignment, the flower that I would pluck
And put between my breasts, oh (then but beginning
To swell about the blossom) she would long
Till she had such another, and commit it
To the like innocent Cradle, where Phenix-like
They di'd in perfume: on my head no toy
But was her pattern, her affections pretty
Though happily, her careless, were, I followed
For my most serious decking, had mine ear
Stol'n some new air, or at adventure humm'd on
From musical Coynage, why, it was a Note
Whereon her spirits would sojourn (rather dwell on)
And sing it in her slumbers; This rehearsal
(Which fury innocent wots well) comes in
Like old importments-bastard, has this end;
That the true love 'tween Maid, and Maid, may be
More than in sex individual.

HIPPOLITO
Y'are out of breath
And this high speeded-pace, is but to say
That you shall never (like the Maid Flavina)
Love any that's call'd Man.

EMILIA
I'm sure I shall not.

HIPPOLITO
Now alack weak Sister,
I must no more believe thee in this point

(Though in't I know thou dost believe thy self)
Then I will trust a sickly appetite,
That loaths even as it longs, but sure my Sister
If I were ripe for your perswasion, you
Have said enough to shake me from the Arm
Of the all noble Theseus, for whose fortunes,
I will now in, and kneel with great assurance,
That we, more than his Pirathous, possess
The high Throne in his heart.

EMILIA
I am not against your faith,
Yet I continue mine.

[Exeunt Cornets.

SCÆNA QUARTA

A Battel struck within: then a Retreat: Flourish. Then enter **THESEUS**, the victor, the **THREE QUEENS**
meet him, and fall on their faces before him.

1ST QUEEN
To thee no Star be dark.

2ND QUEEN
Both Heaven and Earth
Friend thee for ever.

3RD QUEEN
All the good that may
Be wish'd upon thy head, I cry Amen to't.

THESEUS
Th' impartial gods, who from the mounted heavens
View us their mortal Herd, behold who erre,
And in their time chastise: goe and find out
The bones of your dead Lords, and honor them
With treble ceremony, rather than a gap
Should be in their dear rights, we would supply't.
But those we will depute, which shall invest
You in your dignities, and even each thing
Our haste does leave imperfect; So adieu
And heavens good eyes look on you, what are those?

[Exeunt **QUEENS**.

HERALD

Men of great quality, as may be judg'd
By their appointment; some of Thebs have told's
They are Sisters children, Nephews to the King.

THESEUS

By th' Helme of Mars, I saw them in the War,
Like to a pair of Lions, smear'd with prey,
Make lanes in troops agast. I fixt my note
Constantly on them; for they were a mark
Worth a god's view: what prisoner was't that told me
When I enquir'd their names?

HERALD

We leave, they'r called
Arcite and Palamon.

THESEUS

'Tis right, those, those
They are not dead?

[Three Hearses ready.

HERALD

Nor in a state of life, had they been taken
When their last hurts were given, 'twas possible
They might have been recover'd; Yet they breathe
And have the name of men.

THESEUS

Then like men use 'em
The very lees of such (millions of rates)
Exceed the Wine of others, all our Surgeons
Convent in their behoof, our richest balmes
Rather than niggard waste, their lives concern us,
Much more than Thebs is worth, rather than have 'em
Freed of this plight, and in their morning state
(Sound and at liberty) I would 'em dead,
But forty thousand fold, we had rather have 'em
Prisoners to us, than death; bear 'em speedily
From our kind air, to them unkind, and minister
What man to man may do for our sake more,
Since I have known frights, fury, friends, beheasts,
Loves, provocations, zeal, a Mistriss taske,
Desire of liberty, a feavor, madness,
Hath set a mark which nature could not reach too
Without some imposition, sickness in Will
Or wrestling strength in reason, for our Love

And great Apollos mercy, all our best,
Their best skill tender. Lead into the City,
Where having bound things scatter'd, we will post.

[Flourish.

To Athens for our Army.

[Exeunt. Musick.

SCÆNA QUINTA

Enter the **QUEENS**, with the Hearses of their **KNIGHTS**, in a Funeral Solemnity, &c.

Urns and Odours, bring away,
Vapors, sighs, darken the day;
Our dole more deadly looks, than dying
Balmes, and Gumms, and heavy cheers,
Sacred vials fill'd with tears,
And clamors, through the wild air flying:
Come all sad and solemn Shows,
That are quick-ey'd pleasures foes;
We convent nought else but woes.
We convent, &c.

3ᴿᴰ QUEEN
This funeral path, brings to your housholds grave:
Joy seize on you again: peace, sleep with him.

2ᴺᴰ QUEEN
And this to yours.

1ˢᵀ QUEEN
Yours this way: Heavens lend
A thousand differing ways to one sure end.

3ᴿᴰ QUEEN
This world's a City full of straying streets,
And Death's the Market-place, where each one meets.

[Exeunt severally.

ACTUS SECUNDUS

SCÆNA PRIMA

Enter **JAILER** and **WOOER**.

JAILER
I may depart with little, while I live, something I
May cast to you, not much: Alas the Prison I
Keep, though it be for great ones, yet they seldom
Come; before one Salmon, you shall take a number
Of Minnows: I am given out to be better lin'd
Than it can appear, to me report is a true
Speaker: I would I were really, that I am
Deliver'd to be: Marry, what I have (be it what
It will) I will assure upon my daughter at
The day of my death.

WOOER
Sir, I demand no more than your own offer,
And I will estate your Daughter, in what I
Have promised.

JAILER
Well, we will talk more of this, when the solemnity
Is past; But have you a full promise of her?

[Enter **DAUGHTER**.

When that shall be seen, I tender my consent.

WOOER
I have Sir; here she comes.

JAILER
Your friend and I have chanced to name
You here, upon the old business: but no more of that.
Now, so soon as the Court-hurry is over, we will
Have an end of it: I' th' mean time look tenderly
To the two prisoners. I can tell you they are Princes.

DAUGHTER
These strewings are for their Chamber; 'tis pity they
Are in prison, and 'twere pity they should be out: I
Do think they have patience to make any adversity
Asham'd; the prison it self is proud of 'em; and
They have all the world in their Chamber.

JAILER
They are fam'd to be a pair of absolute men.

DAUGHTER
By my troth, I think Fame but stammers 'em, they
Stand a grief above the reach of report.

JAILER
I heard them reported in the battel, to be the only doers.

DAUGHTER
Nay, most likely, for they are noble sufferers; I
Marvel how they would have look'd, had they been
Victors, that with such a constant Nobility, enforce
A freedom out of bondage, making misery their
Mirth, and affliction a toy to jest at.

JAILER
Doe they so?

DAUGHTER
It seems to me, they have no more sence of their
Captivity, than I of ruling Athens: they eat
Well, look merrily, discourse of many things,
But nothing of their own restraint, and disasters:
Yet sometime a divided sigh, martyr'd as 'twere
I' th' deliverance, will break from one of them,
When the other presently gives it so sweet a rebuke,
That I could wish my self a sigh to be so chid,
Or at least a sigher to be comforted.

WOOER
I never saw 'em.

JAILER
The Duke himself came privately in the night.

[Enter **PALAMON** and **ARCITE** above.

And so did they, what the reason of it is, I
Know not: Look, yonder they are; that's
Arcite looks out.

DAUGHTER
No Sir, no, that's Palamon: Arcite is the
Lower of the twain; you may perceive a part
Of him.

JAILER
Go to, leave your pointing; they would not

Make us their object; out of their sight.

DAUGHTER
It is a holliday to look on them: Lord, the
Difference of men.

[Exeunt.

SCÆNA SECUNDA

Enter **PALAMON** and **ARCITE** in prison.

PALAMON
How do you, Noble Cosin?

ARCITE
How do you, Sir?

PALAMON
Why, strong enough to laugh at misery,
And bear the chance of war yet, we are prisoners
I fear for ever Cosin.

ARCITE
I believe it,
And to that destiny have patiently
Laid up my hour to come.

PALAMON
Oh Cosin Arcite,
Where is Thebs now? where is our noble Countrey?
Where are our friends, and kindreds? never more
Must we behold those comforts, never see
The hardy youths strive for the Games of honor
(Hung with the painted favours of their Ladies)
Like tall Ships under Sail: then start amongst 'em
And as an Eastwind leave 'em all behind us,
Like lazy Clouds, whilst Palamon and Arcite,
Even in the wagging of a wanton leg
Out-stript the peoples praises, won the Garlands,
E'r they have time to wish 'em ours. Oh never
Shall we two exercise, like twins of honor,
Our Arms again, and feel our fiery horses,
Like proud Seas under us, our good Swords, now
(Better the red-ey'd god of War nev'r were)
Bravish'd our sides, like age, must run to rust,

And deck the Temples of those gods that hate us,
These hands shall never draw 'em out like light'ning
To blast whole Armies more.

ARCITE
No Palamon,
Those hopes are prisoners with us, here we are
And here the graces of our youths must wither
Like a too-timely Spring; here age must find us,
And which is heaviest (Palamon) unmarried,
The sweet embraces of a loving wife
Loaden with kisses, arm'd with thousand Cupids
Shall never claspe our necks, no issue know us,
No figures of our selves shall we ev'r see,
To glad our age, and like young Eagles teach 'em
Boldly to gaze against bright arms, and say
Remember what your Fathers were, and conquer.
The fair-ey'd Maids, shall weep our banishments,
And in their Songs, curse ever-blinded fortune
Till she for shame see what a wrong she has done
To youth and nature; This is all our world;
We shall know nothing here, but one another,
Hear nothing, but the clock that tels our woes.
The Vine shall grow, but we shall never see it:
Summer shall come, and with her all delights;
But dead-cold winter must inhabit here still.

PALAMON
'Tis too true Arcite
To our Theban hounds,
That shook the aged Forrest with their ecchoes,
No more now must we hollo, no more shake
Our pointed Javelins, whilst the angry Swine
Flies like a Parthian quiver from our rages,
Struck with our well-steel'd Darts: All valiant uses,
(The food and nourishment of noble minds,)
In us two here shall perish; we shall die
(Which is the curse of honor) lastly,
Children of grief, and Ignorance.

ARCITE
Yet Cosin,
Even from the bottom of these miseries
From all that fortune can inflict upon us,
I see two comforts rising, two meer blessings,
If the gods please, to hold here a brave patience,
And the enjoying of our griefs together.
Whilst Palamon is with me, let me perish

If I think this our prison.

PALAMON
Certainly,
'Tis a main goodness, Cosin, that our fortunes
Were twin'd together; 'tis most true, two souls
Put in two noble bodies, let 'em suffer
The gaul of hazard, so they grow together,
Will never sink, they must not, say they could,
A willing man dies sleeping, and all's done.

ARCITE
Shall we make worthy uses of this place
That all men hate so much?

PALAMON
How gentle Cosin?

ARCITE
Let's think this prison, Holy Sanctuary,
To keep us from corruption of worse men,
We are young, and yet desire the wayes of honour,
That liberty and common conversation,
The poison of pure spirits, might, like women,
Wooe us to wander from. What worthy blessing
Can be but our imaginations
May make it ours? And here being thus together,
We are an endless mine to one another;
We are one anothers Wife, ever begetting
New births of love; we are Father, Friends, Acquaintance,
We are, in one another, Families,
I am your Heir, and you are mine: This place
Is our Inheritance: no hard oppressor
Dare take this from us; here with a little patience
We shall live long, and loving: No surfeits seek us:
The hand of War hurts none here, nor the Seas
Swallow their youth: were we at liberty,
A Wife might part us lawfully, or business,
Quarrels consume us: Envy of ill men
Crave our acquaintance, I might sicken Cosin,
Where you should never know it, and so perish
Without your noble hand to close mine eyes,
Or prayers to the gods; a thousand chances
Were we from hence, would sever us.

PALAMON
You have made me
(I thank you Cosin Arcite) almost wanton

With my Captivity: what a misery
It is to live abroad! and every where:
'Tis like a Beast me thinks: I find the Court here,
I 'm sure a more content, and all those pleasures
That wooe the Wills of men to vanity,
I see through now; and am sufficient
To tell the world, 'tis but a gaudy shadow,
That old Time, as he passes by, takes with him,
What had we been old in the Court of Creon,
Where sin is Justice, Lust, and Ignorance,
The virtues of the great ones: Cosin Arcite
Had not the loving gods found this place for us
We had di'd as they doe, ill old men unwept,
And had their Epitaphs, the peoples Curses,
Shall I say more?

ARCITE
I would hear you still.

PALAMON
Ye shall.
Is there record of any two that lov'd
Better than we two Arcite?

ARCITE
Sure there cannot.

PALAMON
I doe not think it possible our friendship
Should ever leave us.

ARCITE
Till our deaths it cannot.

[Enter **EMILIA** and her **WOMAN**.

And after death our spirits shall be led
To those that love eternally. Speak on Sir.
This Garden has a world of pleasures in't.

EMILIA
What Flower is this?

WOMAN
'Tis call'd Narcissus, Madam.

EMILIA
That was a fair Boy certain, but a fool,

To love himself, were there not Maids enough?

ARCITE
Pray forward.

PALAMON
Yes.

EMILIA
Or were they all hard-hearted?

WOMAN
They could not be to one so fair.

EMILIA
Thou wouldst not.

WOMAN
I think I should not, Madam.

EMILIA
That's a good wench:
But take heed to your kindness though.

WOMAN
Why Madam?

EMILIA
Men are mad things.

ARCITE
Will ye go forward, Cosin?

EMILIA
Canst not thou work such Flowers in Silk wench?

WOMAN
Yes.

EMILIA
I'll have a Gown full of 'em, and of these,
This is a pretty colour, wil't not do
Rarely upon a skirt wench?

WOMAN
Dainty Madam.

ARCITE

Cosin, Cosin, how do you, Sir? Why Palamon?

PALAMON
Never till now, I was in prison Arcite.

ARCITE
Why, what's the matter man?

PALAMON
Behold, and wonder.
By heaven she is a Goddess.

ARCITE
Ha.

PALAMON
Do reverence.
She is a Goddess Arcite.

EMILIA
Of all Flowers,
Methinks a Rose is best.

WOMAN
Why gentle Madam?

EMILIA
It is the very Emblem of a Maid.
For when the West wind courts her gently
How modestly she blows, and paints the Sun,
With her chaste blushes! When the North comes near her,
Rude and impatient, then like Chastity
She locks her beauties in her bud again,
And leaves him to base briers.

WOMAN
Yet good Madam,
Sometimes her modesty will blow so far
She falls for't: a Maid
If she have any honor, would be loth
To take example by her.

EMILIA
Thou art wanton.

ARCITE
She is wondrous fair.

PALAMON
She is all the beauty extant.

EMILIA
The Sun grows high, let's walk in, keep these flowers,
We'll see how near Art can come near their colours;
I'm wondrous merry-hearted, I could laugh now.

WOMAN
I could lie down I am sure.

EMILIA
And take one with you?

WOMAN
That's as we bargain, Madam.

EMILIA
Well, agree then.

[Exeunt **EMILIA** and **WOMAN**.

PALAMON
What think you of this beauty?

ARCITE
'Tis a rare one.

PALAMON
Is't but a rare one?

ARCITE
Yes, a matchless beauty.

PALAMON
Might not a man well lose himself, and love her?

ARCITE
I cannot tell what you have done, I have,
Beshrew mine eyes for't, now I feel my Shackles.

PALAMON
You love her then?

ARCITE
Who would not?

PALAMON

And desire her?

ARCITE
Before my liberty.

PALAMON
I saw her first.

ARCITE
That's nothing.

PALAMON
But it shall be.

ARCITE
I saw her too.

PALAMON
Yes, but you must not love her.

ARCITE
I will not as you do; to worship her;
As she is heavenly, and a blessed goddess;
(I love her as a woman, to enjoy her)
So both may love.

PALAMON
You shall not love at all.

ARCITE
Not love at all;
Who shall denie me?

PALAMON
I that first saw her; I that took possession
First with mine eye of all those beauties
In her reveal'd to mankind: if thou lov'st her;
Or entertain'st a hope to blast my wishes,
Thou art a Traitor Arcite, and a fellow
False as thy Title to her: friendship, bloud
And all the ties between us I disclaim
If thou once think upon her.

ARCITE
Yes, I love her,
And if the lives of all my name lay on it,
I must do so, I love her with my soul,
If that will lose ye, farewel Palamon.

I say again, I love, and in loving her, maintain
I am as worthy and as free a Lover
And have as just a title to her beauty
As any Palamon, or any living
That is a mans Son.

PALAMON

Have I call'd thee friend?

ARCITE

Yes, and have found me so; why are you mov'd thus?
Let me deal coldly with you, am not I
Part of your blood, part of your soul? you have told me
That I was Palamon, and you were Arcite.

PALAMON

Yes.

ARCITE

Am not I liable to those affections,
Those joyes, griefs, angers, fears, my friend shall suffer?

PALAMON

Ye may be.

ARCITE

Why then would you deal so cunningly,
So strangely, so unlike a Noble Kinsman
To love alone? speak truly, do you think me
Unworthy of her sight?

PALAMON

No, but unjust,
If thou pursue that sight.

ARCITE

Because another
First sees the Enemy, shall I stand still
And let mine honor down, and never charge?

PALAMON

Yes, if he be but one.

ARCITE

But say that one
Had rather combat me?

PALAMON

Let that one say so,
And use thy freedom: else if thou pursuest her,
Be as that cursed man that hates his Countrey,
A branded villain.

ARCITE
You are mad.

PALAMON
I must be.
Till thou art worthy, Arcite, it concerns me,
And in this madness, if I hazard thee
And take thy life, I deal but truly.

ARCITE
Fie Sir.
You play the child extreamly: I will love her,
I must, I ought to do so, and I dare,
And all this justly.

PALAMON
Oh that now, that now
Thy false-self, and thy friend, had but this fortune
To be one hour at liberty, and graspe
Our good swords in our hands, I would quickly teach thee
What 'twere to filch affection from another:
Thou art baser in it than a Cutpurse;
Put but thy head out of this window more,
And as I have a soul, I'll nail thy life to't.

ARCITE
Thou dar'st not fool, thou canst not, thou art feeble.
Put my head out? I'll throw my Body out,
And leap the Garden, when I see her next.

[Enter **KEEPER**.

And pitch between her Arms to anger thee.

PALAMON
No more; the Keepers coming; I shall live
To knock thy brains out with my Shackles.

ARCITE
Doe.

KEEPER
By your leave, Gentlemen.

PALAMON
Now honest Keeper?

KEEPER
Lord Arcite, you must presently to th' Duke;
The cause I know not yet.

ARCITE
I am ready Keeper.

KEEPER
Prince Palamon, I must awhile bereave you
Of your fair Cosins company.

[Exeunt **ARCITE** and **KEEPER**.

PALAMON
And me too,
Even when you please of life; why is he sent for?
It may be he shall marry her, he's goodly,
And like enough the Duke hath taken notice
Both of his Bloud and Body: but his falshood,
Why should a friend be treacherous? if that
Get him a Wife so noble, and so fair;
Let honest men ne'er love again. Once more
I would but see this fair one: blessed Garden,
And Fruit, and Flowers more blessed that still blossom
As her bright eies shine on ye. Would I were
For all the fortune of my life hereafter
Yon little Tree, yon blooming Apricock;
How I would spread, and fling my wanton arms
In at her window; I would bring her fruit
Fit for the gods to feed on: youth and pleasure
Still as she tasted should be doubled on her,
And if she be not heavenly, I would make her
So near the gods in nature, they should fear her.

[Enter **KEEPER**.

And then I'm sure she would love me: how now Keeper,
Where's Arcite?

KEEPER
Banish'd: Prince Pirithous
Obtain'd his liberty; but never more
Upon his oath and life must he set foot
Upon this Kingdom.

PALAMON
He's a blessed man,
He shall see Thebes again, and call to Arms
The bold young men, that when he bids 'em charge,
Fall on like fire: Arcite shall have a Fortune,
If he dare make himself a worthy Lover,
Yet in the Field to strike a battel for her;
And if he lose her then, he's a cold Coward;
How bravely may he bear himself to win her
If he be noble Arcite; thousand ways.
Were I at liberty, I would do things
Of such a virtuous greatness, that this Lady,
This blushing Virgin should take manhood to her
And seek to ravish me.

KEEPER
My Lord for you
I have this charge too.

PALAMON
To discharge my life.

KEEPER
No, but from this place to remove your Lordship,
The windows are too open.

PALAMON
Devils take 'em
That are so envious to me; prethee kill me.

KEEPER
And hang for't afterward.

PALAMON
By this good light
Had I a sword I would kill thee.

KEEPER
Why my Lord?

PALAMON
Thou bring'st such pelting scurvy news continually
Thou art not worthy life; I will not go.

KEEPER
Indeed you must my Lord.

PALAMON
May I see the Garden?

KEEPER
No.

PALAMON
Then I am resolv'd, I will not go.

KEEPER
I must constrain you then: and, for you are dangerous
I'll clap more irons on you.

PALAMON
Doe good Keeper.
I'll shake 'em so, ye shall not sleep,
I'll make ye a new Morrisse, must I goe?

KEEPER
There is no remedy.

PALAMON
Farewel kind window.
May rude wind never hurt thee. Oh my Lady,
If ever thou hast felt what sorrow was,
Dream how I suffer. Come; now bury me.

[Exeunt **PALAMON** and **KEEPER**.

SCÆNA TERTIA

Enter **ARCITE**.

ARCITE
Banish'd the Kingdom? 'tis a benefit,
A mercy I must thank 'em for, but banish'd
The free enjoying of that face I die for,
Oh 'twas a studdied punishment, a death
Beyond Imagination: Such a vengeance
That were I old and wicked, all my sins
Could never pluck upon me, Palamon;
Thou hast the Start now, thou shalt stay and see
Her bright eyes break each morning 'gainst thy window,
And let in life into thee; Thou shalt feed
Upon the sweetness of a noble beauty,
That nature never exceeded, nor never shall:

Good gods! what happiness has Palamon!
Twenty to one, he'll come to speak to her,
And if she be as gentle, as she's fair,
I know she's his, he has a Tongue will tame
Tempests, and make the wild Rocks wanton.
Come what can come,
The worst is death; I will not leave the Kingdom,
I know mine own is but a heap of ruins,
And no redress there, if I go, he has her,
I 'm resolv'd an other shape shall make me,
Or end my fortunes. Either way, I' m happy:
I'll see her, and be near her, or no more.

[Enter **FOUR COUNTRY-PEOPLE**, & one with a garland before them.

1ST COUNTRY-PERSON
My Masters, I'll be there that's certain.

2ND COUNTRY-PERSON
And I'll be there.

3RD COUNTRY-PERSON
And I.

4TH COUNTRY-PERSON
Why then have with ye Boys; 'Tis but a chiding,
Let the plough play to day, I'll tick' It out
Of the jades tails to morrow.

1ST COUNTRY-PERSON
I 'm sure
To have my wife as jealous as a Turkey:
But that's all one, I'll goe through, let her mumble.

2ND COUNTRY-PERSON
Clap her aboard to morrow night, and stoa her,
And all's made up again.

3RD COUNTRY-PERSON
I, do but put a fesku in her fist, and you shall see her
Take a new lesson out, and be a good wench.
Doe we all hold, against the Maying?

4TH COUNTRY-PERSON
Hold? what should ail us?

3RD COUNTRY-PERSON
Arcas, will be there.

2ᴺᴰ COUNTRY-PERSON
And Sennois.
And Rycas, and 3. Better lads never danc'd under green Tree,
And yet know what wenches: ha?
But will the dainty Domine, the Schoolemaster keep touch
Doe you think: For he do's all ye know.

3ᴿᴰ COUNTRY-PERSON
He'll eat a hornbook ere he fail: goe too, the matter's
too far driven between him, and the Tanners daughter, to let
slip now, and she must see the Duke, and she must dance too.

4ᵀᴴ COUNTRY-PERSON
Shall we be lusty.

2ᴺᴰ COUNTRY-PERSON
All the Boys in Athens blow wind i'th' breech on's, and
here I'll be and there I'll be, for our Town, and here again,
and there again: Ha, Boys, heigh for the weavers.

1ˢᵀ COUNTRY-PERSON
This must be done i'th woods.

4ᵀᴴ COUNTRY-PERSON
O pardon me.

2ᴺᴰ COUNTRY-PERSON
By any means our thing of learning sees so: Where he
himself will edifie the Duke most parlously in our behalfs:
He's excellent i'th' woods, bring him to'th' plains, his
learning makes no cry.

3ᴿᴰ COUNTRY-PERSON
We'll see the sports, then every man to's Tackle: and
Sweet Companions lets rehearse by any means, before
The Ladies see us, and doe sweetly, and God knows what
May come on't.

4ᵀᴴ COUNTRY-PERSON
Content; the sports once ended, we'll perform. Away
Boys and hold.

ARCITE
By your leaves honest friends: Pray you whither goe you.

4ᵀᴴ COUNTRY-PERSON
Whither? Why, what a question's that!

ARCITE
Yes, 'tis a question, to me that know not.

3RD COUNTRY-PERSON
To the Games, my Friend.

2ND COUNTRY-PERSON
Where were you bred you know it not?

ARCITE
Not far Sir,
Are there such Games, to day?

1ST COUNTRY-PERSON
Yes marry are there:
And such as you never saw; The Duke, himself
Will be in person there.

ARCITE
What pastimes are they?

2ND COUNTRY-PERSON
Wrastling, and Running; 'Tis a pretty Fellow.

3RD COUNTRY-PERSON
Thou wilt not goe along.

ARCITE
Not yet Sir.

4TH COUNTRY-PERSON
Well Sir
Take your own time, come Boys.

1ST COUNTRY-PERSON
My mind misgives me
This fellow has a veng'ance trick o'th hip,
Marke how his Bodi's made for't.

2ND COUNTRY-PERSON
I'll be hang'd though
If he dare venture, hang him plumb-porredge,
He wrestle? He rost eggs. Come lets be gon Lads.

[Exeunt **FOUR COUNTRY-PEOPLE**.

ARCITE

.....is is an offer'd oportunity
I durst not wish for. Well, I could have wrestled,
The best men call'd it excellent, and run
Swifter, than wind upon a feild of Corn
(Curling the wealthy ears) never flew: I'll venture,
And in some poor disguize be there, who knows
Whether my brows may not be girt with garlands?
And happiness prefer me to a place,
Where I may ever dwell in sight of her.

[Exit **ARCITE**.

SCÆNA QUARTA

Enter Jailors **DAUGHTER** alone.

DAUGHTER
Why should I love this Gentleman? 'Tis odds
He never will affect me; I am base,
My Father the mean Keeper of his Prison,
And he a Prince; To marry him is hopeless;
To be his whore, is witles; Out upon't;
What pushes are we wenches driven to
When fifteen once has found us? First I saw him,
I (seeing) thought he was a goodly man;
He has as much to please a woman in him,
(If he please to bestow it so) as ever
These eyes yet lookt on; Next, I pittied him,
And so would any young wench o'my Conscience
That ever dream'd, or vow'd her Maydenhead
To a young hansom Man; Then I lov'd him,
(Extremely lov'd him) infinitely lov'd him;
And yet he had a Cosen, fair as he too.
But in my heart was Palamon, and there
Lord, what a coyl he keepes! To hear him
Sing in an evening, what a Heaven it is!
And yet his Songs are sad-ones; Fairer spoken,
Was never Gentleman. When I come in
To bring him water in a morning, first
He bows his noble body, then salutes me, thus:
Fair, gentle Mayd, good morrow, may thy goodness,
Get thee a happy husband; Once he kist me,
I lov'd my lips the better ten daies after,
Would he would doe so ev'ry day; He greives much,
And me as much to see his misery:
What should I doe, to make him know I love him,

For I would fain enjoy him? Say I ventur'd
To set him free? What saies the Law then? Thus much
For Law, or kindred: I will doe it,
And this night, or to morrow he shall love me.

[Exit.

[This short flourish of Cornets and Showtes within.

SCÆNA QUINTA

Enter **THESEUS, HIPPOLITA, PERITHOUS, EMILIA: ARCITE** with a Garland, &c.

THESEUS
You have done worthily; I have not seen
Since Hercules, a man of tougher sinews;
What ere you are, you run the best, and wrestle,
That these times can allow.

ARCITE
I'm proud to please you.

THESEUS
What Countrie bred you?

ARCITE
This; But far off, Prince.

THESEUS
Are you a Gentleman?

ARCITE
My father said so;
And to those gentle uses gave me life.

THESEUS
Are you his heir?

ARCITE
His youngest Sir.

THESEUS
Your Father
Sure is a happy Sire, then: What proves you?

ARCITE

A little of all noble Qualities:
I could have kept a Hawk, and well have hollow'd
To a deep crie of Dogs; I dare not praise
My feat in horsemanship: yet they that knew me
Would say it was my best peece: last, and greatest,
I would be thought a Soldier.

THESEUS
You are perfect.

PERITHOUS
Upon my soul, a proper man.

EMILIA
He is so.

PERITHOUS
How doe you like him Ladie?

HIPPOLITO
I admire him,
I have not seen so young a man, so noble
(If he say true,) of his sort.

EMILIA
Believe,
His mother was a wondrous handsome woman,
His face me thinks, goes that way.

HIPPOLITO
But his Body
And firie mind, illustrate a brave Father.

PERITHOUS
Mark how his virtue, like a hidden Sun,
Breaks through his baser garments.

HIPPOLITO
He's well got sure.

THESEUS
What made you seek this place Sir?

ARCITE
Noble Theseus.
To purchase name, and doe my ablest service
To such a well-found wonder, as thy worth,
For only in thy Court, of all the world

Dwells fair-ey'd honor.

PERITHOUS
All his words are worthy.

THESEUS
Sir, we are much endebted to your travell,
Nor shall you loose your wish: Perithous
Dispose of this faire Gentleman.

PERITOHUS
Thanks Theseus.
What ere you are y'are mine, and I shall give you
To a most noble service, to this Lady,
This bright young Virgin; Pray observe her goodness;
You have honour'd her fair birth-day, with your virtues,
And as your due y'are hers: kiss her fair hand Sir.

ARCITE
Sir, y'are a noble Giver: dearest Beautie,
Thus let me seal my vow'd faith: when your Servant
(Your most unworthie Creature) but offends you,
Command him die, he shall.

EMILIA
That were too cruell.
If you deserve well Sir; I shall soon see't:
Y'are mine, and somewhat better than your ranck I'll use you.

PERITHOUS
I'll see you furnish'd, and because you say
You are a horseman, I must needs intreat you
This after noon to ride, but 'tis a rough one.

ARCITE
I like him better (Prince) I shall not then
Freeze in my Saddle.

THESEUS
Sweet, you must be readie,
And you Emilia, and you (Friend) and all
To morrow by the Sun, to doe observance
To flowry May, in Dian's wood: wait well Sir,
Upon your Mistris: Emely, I hope
He shall not goe a foot.

EMILIA
That were a shame Sir,

While I have horses: take your choice, and what
You want at any time, let me but know it;
If you serve faithfully, I dare assure you
You'll find a loving Mistris.

ARCITE
If I doe not,
Let me find that my Father ever hated,
Disgrace, and blows.

THESEUS
Go lead the way; You have won it:
It shall be so; You shall receive all dues
Fit for the honor you have won; 'Twere wrong else.
Sister, beshrew my heart, you have a Servant,
That if I were a woman, would be Master,
But you are wise.

[Flourish.

EMILIA
I hope too wise for that Sir.

[Exeunt **OMNES**.

SCÆNA SEXTA

Enter Jailor's **DAUGHTER** alone.

DAUGHTER
Let all the Dukes, and all the divells rore,
He is at liberty: I have ventur'd for him:
And out I have brought him to a little wood
A mile hence, I have sent him, where a Cedar,
Higher than all the rest, spreads like a plane
Fast by a Brook, and there he shall keep close,
Till I provide him Fyles, and food; for yet
His yron bracelets are not off. O Love
What a stout hearted child thou art! My Father
Durst better have indur'd cold iron, than done it:
I love him beyond love, and beyond reason,
Or wit, or safetie: I have made him know it
I care not, I am desperate: If the Law
Find me, and then condemne me for't; Some wenches,
Some honest hearted Maids, will sing my Dirge.
And tell to memory, my death was noble,

Dying almost a Martyr: That way he takes,
I purpose is my way too: Sure he cannot
Be so unmanly, as to leave me here,
If he doe, Maids will not so easily
Trust men again: And yet he has not thank'd me
For what I have done: no not so much as kist me,
And that (me thinks) is not so well; Nor scarcely
Could I persuade him to become a Freeman,
He made such scruples of the wrong he did
To me, and to my Father. Yet I hope
When he considers more, this love of mine
Will take more root within him: Let him doe
What he will with me, so he use me kindly,
For use me so he shall, or I'll proclaim him,
And to his face, no man: I'll presently
Provide him necessaries, and pack my cloaths up,
And where there is a path of ground I'll venture
So he be with me; By him, like a shadow
I'll ever dwell; Within this hour the whoobub
Will be all o'er the prison: I am then
Kissing the man they look for: Farewell Father,
Get many more such prisoners, and such daughters,
And shortly you may keep your self. Now to him:

[Cornets in sundry places. Noise and hollowing as **PEOPLE** a Maying.

ACTUS TERTIUS

SCÆNA PRIMA

Enter **ARCITE** alone.

ARCITE
The Duke has lost Hypolita; Each took
A severall land. This is a solemn Right
They owe bloom'd May, and the Athenians pay it
To 'th' heart of Ceremony: O Queen Emilia
Fresher than May, sweeter
Then her gold Buttons on the bows, or all
Th'enamell'd knacks o'th' Mead, or garden, yea
(We challenge too) the banck of any Nymph
That makes the stream seem flowers; Thou o Jewell
O'th wood, o'th world, hast likewise blest a pace
With thy sole presence, in thy rumination
That I poor man might eftsoones come betwen
And chop on some cold thought, thrice blessed chance

To drop on such a Mistris, expectation
Most guiltless on't: tell me O Lady Fortune
(Next after Emely my Sovereign) how far
I may be proud. She takes strong note of me,
Hath made me near her; and this beauteous Morn
(The prim'st of all the year) presents me with
A brace of horses, two such Steeds might well
Be by a pair of Kings backt, in a Field
That their crowns titles tried: Alas, alas
Poor Cosen Palamon, poor prisoner, thou
So little dream'st upon my fortune, that
Thou thinkst thy self, the happier thing, to be
So near Emilia, me thou deem'st at Thebs,
And therein wretched, although free; But if
Thou knew'st my Mistris breath'd on me, and that
I ear'd her language, liv'd in her eye; O Coz
What passion would enclose thee.

[Enter **PALAMON** as out of a Bush, with his Shackles: bends his fist at **ARCITE**.

PALAMON
Traytor kinsman,
Thou shouldst perceive my passion, if these signs
Of prisonment were off me, and this hand
But owner of a Sword: By all oaths in one
I, and the justice of my love would make thee
A confest Traytor: O thou most perfidious
That ever gently look'd the voydes of honor.
That ev'r bore gentle Token; falsest Cosen
That ever blood made kin, call'st thou her thine?
I'll prove it in my Shackles, with these hands,
Void of appointment, that thou ly'st, and art
A very theef in love, a Chaffy Lord
Nor worth the name of villain: had I a Sword
And these house cloggs away.

ARCITE
Dear Cosin Palamon.

PALAMON
Cosoner Arcite, give me language, such
As thou hast shew'd me feat.

ARCITE
Not finding in
The circuit of my breast, any gross stuff
To form me like your blazon, holds me to
This gentleness of answer; 'tis your passion

That thus mistakes, the which to you being enemy,
Cannot to me be kind: honor, and honestie
I cherish, and depend on, how so ev'r
You skip them in me, and with them fair Coz
I'll maintain my proceedings; pray be pleas'd
To shew in generous terms, your griefs, since that
Your question's with your equall, who professes
To clear his own way, with the mind and Sword
Of a true Gentleman.

PALAMON
That thou durst Arcite.

ARCITE
My Coz, my Coz, you have been well advertis'd
How much I dare, y'ave seen me use my Sword
Against th' advice of fear: sure of another
You would not hear me doubted, but your silence
Should break out, though i'th' Sanctuary.

PALAMON
Sir,
I have seen you move in such a place, which well
Might justifie your manhood, you were call'd
A good knight and a bold; But the whole week's not fair
If any day it rayn: Their valiant temper
Men loose when they encline to trecherie,
And then they fight like coupel'd Beeres, would fly
Were they not ty'd.

ARCITE
Kinsman, you might as well
Speak this, and act it in your Glass, as to
His ear, which now disdains you.

PALAMON
Come up to me,
Quit me of these cold Gyves, give me a Sword
Though it be rustie, and the charity
Of one meal lend me; Come before me then,
A good Sword in thy hand, and doe but say
That Emily is thine, I will forgive
The trespass thou hast done me, yea my life
If then thou carry't, and brave souls in shades
That have di'd manly, which will seek of me
Some news from earth, they shall get none but this,
That thou art brave, and noble.

ARCITE
Be content,
Again betake you to your hawthorn house,
With counsel of the night, I will be here
With wholesome viands; these impediments
Will I file off, you shall have garments, and
Perfumes to kill the smell o'th' prison, after
When you shall stretch your self, and say but Arcite
I am in plight, there shall be at your choice
Both Sword, and Armor.

PALAMON
Oh you heavens, dare any
So noble bear a guilty business! none
But only Arcite, therefore none but Arcite
In this kind is so bold.

ARCITE
Sweet Palamon.

PALAMON
I doe embrace you, and your offer, for
Your offer do't I only, Sir your person
Without hypocrisy I may not wish

[Wind horns of Cornets.

More than my Swords edge ont.

ARCITE
You hear the Horns;
Enter your Musick least this match between's
Be crost e'r met, give me your hand, farewell.
I'll bring you every needfull thing: I pray you
Take comfort and be strong.

PALAMON
Pray hold your promise;
And doe the deed with a bent brow, most certain
You love me not, be rough with me, and pour
This oil out of your language; by this ayr
I could for each word, give a Cuff: my stomach
Not reconcil'd by reason.

ARCITE
Plainly spoken,
Yet pardon me hard language, when I spur

[Wind horns.

My horse, I chide him not; content, and anger
In me have but one face. Hark Sir, they call
The scatter'd to the Banket; you must guess
I have an office there.

PALAMON
Sir your attendance
Cannot please heaven, and I know your office
Unjustly is atcheiv'd.

ARCITE
If a good title,
I'm persuaded this question sick between's,
By bleeding must be cur'd. I'm a Suitor,
That to your Sword you will bequeath this plea,
And talk of it no more.

PALAMON
But this one word:
You are going now to gaze upon my Mistris,
For note you, mine she is.

ARCITE
Nay then.

PALAMON
Nay pray you,
You talk of feeding me to breed me strength
You are going now to look upon a Sun
That strengthens what it looks on, there
You have a vantage o'er me, but enjoy't till
I may enforce my remedy. Farewell.

[Exeunt.

SCÆNA SECUNDA

Enter Jailers **DAUGHTER** alone.

DAUGHTER
He has mistook; the Beak I meant, is gone
After his fancy, 'Tis now welnigh morning,
No matter, would it were perpetuall night,
And darkness Lord o'th' world, Hark 'tis a wolf:

In me hath grief slain fear, and but for one thing
I care for nothing, and that's Palamon.
I wreak not if the wolves would jaw me, so
He had this File; what if I hollow'd for him?
I cannot hollow: if I whoop'd; what then?
If he not answer'd, I should call a wolf,
And doe him but that service. I have heard
Strange howls this live-long night, why may't not be
They have made prey of him? he has no weapons,
He cannot run, the Jengling of his Gives
Might call fell things to listen, who have in them
A sence to know a man unarm'd, and can
Smell where resistance is. I'll set it down
He's torn to peeces, they howl'd many together
And then they fed on him: So much for that,
Be bold to ring the Bell; How stand I then?
All's char'd when he is gone, No, no I lye,
My Father's to be hang'd for his escape,
My self to beg, if I priz'd life so much
As to deny my act, but that I would not,
Should I try death by dussons: I am mop't,
Food took I none these two daies.
Sipt some water, I have not clos'd mine eyes
Save when my lids scowrd off their bine; alas
Dissolve my life, Let not my sence unsettle
Least I should drown, or stab or hang my self.
O state of Nature, fail together in me,
Since thy best props are warpt: So which way now?
The best way is, the next way to a grave:
Each errant step beside is torment. Loe
The Moon is down, the Cr'ckets chirpe, the Schreich-owl
Calls in the dawn; all offices are done
Save what I fail in: But the point is this
An end, and that is all.

[Exit.

SCÆNIA TERTIA

Enter **ARCITE** with Meat, Wine, and Files.

ARCITE
I should be near the place, hoa. Cosen Palamon.

[Enter **PALAMON.**

PALAMON
Arcite?

ARCITE
The same: I have brought you food and files,
Come forth and fear not, here's no Theseus.

PALAMON
Nor none so honest Arcite.

ARCITE
That's no matter,
We'll argue that hereafter: Come take courage,
You shall not dye thus beastly, here Sir drink:
I know you're faint, then I'll talk further with you.

PALAMON
Arcite, thou mightst now poyson me.

ARCITE
I might.
But I must fear you first: Sit down, and good now
No more of these vain parlies; let us not
Having our ancient reputation with us
Make talk for Fools, and Cowards, To your health. &c.

PALAMON
Doe.

ARCITE
Pray sit down then, and let me entreat you
By all the honesty and honor in you,
No mention of this woman, 't will disturb us,
We shall have time enough.

PALAMON
Well Sir, I'll pledge you.

ARCITE
Drinke a good hearty draught, it breeds good blood man.
Doe not you feel it thaw you?

PALAMON
Stay, I'll tell you after a draught or two more.

ARCITE
Spare it not, the Duke has more Cuz: Eat now.

PALAMON
Yes.

ARCITE
I am glad you have so good a stomach.

PALAMON
I am gladder I have so good meat to't.

ARCITE
Is't not mad lodging here in the wild woods Cosen?

PALAMON
Yes, for them that have wild Consciences.

ARCITE
How tasts your victuals? your hunger needs no sawce I see.

PALAMON
Not much.
But if it did, yours is too tart: sweet Cosen: what is this?

ARCITE
Venison.

PALAMON
'Tis a lusty meat:
Give me more wine; here Arcite to the wenches
We have known in our daies. The Lord Stewards daughter.
Doe you remember her?

ARCITE
After you Cuz.

PALAMON
She lov'd a black-hair'd man.

ARCITE
She did so; well Sir.

PALAMON
And I have heard some call him Arcite; an.

ARCITE
Out with't faith.

PALAMON
She met him in an Arbor:

What did she there Cuz? play o'the virginals?

ARCITE
Something she did Sir.

PALAMON
Made her groan a Month for't; or 2. or 3. or 10.

ARCITE
The Marshals Sister,
Had her share too, as I remember Cosen,
Else there be tales abroad, you'll pledge her?

PALAMON
Yes.

ARCITE
A pretty brown wench 'tis: There was a time
When young men went a hunting, and a wood,
And a broad beech: and thereby hangs a tale: heigh ho.

PALAMON
For Emily, upon my life, fool
A way with this strain'd mirth; I say again
That sigh was breath'd for Emily; base Cosen,
Dar'st thou break first?

ARCITE
You are wide.

PALAMON
By heaven and earth, there's nothing in thee honest.

ARCITE
Then I'll leave you: you are a Beast now:

PALAMON
As thou mak'st me, Traytor.

ARCITE
There's all things needfull, files and shirts, and perfumes.
I'll come again some two hours hence, and bring
That that shall quiet all.

PALAMON
A Sword and Armor.

ARCITE

Fear me not; you are now too fowl; farewell.
Get off your Trinkets, you shall want nought.

PALAMON
Sir ha:

ARCITE
I'll here no more.

[Exit.

PALAMON
If he keep touch, he dies for't.

[Exit.

SCÆNA QUARTA

Enter Jailers **DAUGHTER**.

DAUGHTER
I am very cold, and all the Stars are out too,
The little Stars, and all, that look like aglets:
The Sun has seen my Folly: Palamon;
Alas no; he's in heaven; where am I now?
Yonder's the sea, and there's a Ship; how't tumbles
And there's a Rock lies watching under water;
Now, now, it beats upon it; now, now, now,
There's a leak sprung, a sound one, how they cry!
Upon her before the wind, you'll loose all els:
Up with a course or two, and tack about Boys.
Good night, good night, y'are gone; I'm very hungry,
Would I could find a fine Frog; he would tell me
News from all parts o'th' world, then would I make
A Careck of a Cockle-shell, and sayll
By East and North East to the King of Pigmies,
For he tels fortunes rarely. Now my Father
Twenty to one is trust up in a trice
To morrow morning, I'll say never a word.

[Sing.

For I'll cut my green coat, afoot above my knee,
And I'll clip my yellow locks; an inch below mine eie.
hey, nonny, nonny, nonny.

He's buy me a whit Cut, forth for to ride
And I'll goe seek him, throw the world that is so wide.
hey nonny, nonny, nonny.

O for a prick now like a Nightingale, to put my brest
Against. I shall sleep like a Top else.

[Exit.

SCÆNA QUINTA

Enter a **SCHOOLMASTER**, **FOUR COUNTRYMEN**: and **2 or 3 WENCHES, BAUM**, with a **TABORER**.

SCHOOLMASTER
Fy, fy, what tediosity, & disensanity is here among ye? have my Rudiments bin labour'd so long with ye?
milk'd unto ye, and, by a figure, even the very plumbroth & marrow of my understanding laid upon ye?
and do you still cry where, and how, & wherefore? you most course freeze capacities, ye jave
Judgements, have I said thus let be, and there let be, and then let be, and no man understand me, prob
deum, medius fidius, ye are all dunces: For why here stand I. Here the Duke comes, there are you close
in the Thicket; the Duke appears, I meet him, and unto him I utter learned things, and many figures, he
hears, and nods, and hums, and then cries rare, and I goe forward, at length I fling my Cap up; mark
there; then do you as once did Meleager, and the Bore break comely out before him: like true lovers,
cast your selves in a Body decently, and sweetly, by a figure trace, and turn Boys.

1ST COUNTRYMAN
And sweetly we will doe it Master Gerrold.

2ND COUNTRYMAN
Draw up the Company, Where's the Taboror?

3RD COUNTRYMAN
Why Timothy?

TABORER
Here my mad boys, have at ye.

SCHOOLMASTER
But I say where's their women?

4TH COUNTRYMAN
Here's Friz and Maudline.

2ND COUNTRYMAN
And little Luce, with the white legs, and bouncing
Barbary.

1ˢᵀ COUNTRYMAN
And freckled Nel; that never fail'd her Master.

SCHOOLMASTER
Where be your Ribands maids? swym with your Bodies
And carry it sweetly, and deliverly
And now and then a favor, and a friske.

NEL
Let us alone Sir.

SCHOOLMASTER
Where's the rest o'th' Musick.

3ᴿᴰ COUNTRYMAN
Dispers'd as you commanded.

SCHOOLMASTER
Couple then
And see what's wanting; where's the Bavian?
My friend, carry your tail without offence
Or scandall to the Ladies; and be sure
You tumble with audacity, and manhood,
And when you bark doe it with judgement.

BAUM
Yes Sir.

SCHOOLMASTER
Quo usque tandem? Here is a woman wanting.

4ᵀᴴ COUNTRYMAN
We may goe whistle: all the fat's i'th' fire.

SCHOOLMASTER
We have,
As learned Authors utter, wash'd a Tile,
We have been fatuus, and labour'd vainly.

2ᴺᴰ COUNTRYMAN
This is that scornfull peece, that scurvy hilding
That gave her promise faithfully, she would be here,
Cicely the Sempsters daughter:
The next gloves that I give her shall be dogs-skin;
Nay and she fail me once, you can tell Arcas,
She swore by wine, and bread, she would not break.

SCHOOLMASTER

An Eel and woman,
A learned Poet sayes: unles by'th' tail
And with thy teeth thou hold, will either fail,
In manners this was false position.

1ˢᵀ COUNTRYMAN
A fire ill take her; do's she flinch now?

3ᴿᴰ COUNTRYMAN
What
Shall we determine Sir?

SCHOOLMASTER
Nothing,
Our business is become a nullity
Yea, and a woefull, and a pittious nullity.

4ᵀᴴ COUNTRYMAN
Now when the credit of our Town lay on it,
Now to be frampall, now to piss o'th' nettle,
Goe thy ways, I'll remember thee, I'll fit thee.

[Enter Jailer's **DAUGHTER**.

Daughter,
The George alow, came from the South, from
The coast of Barbary a.
And there he met with brave gallants of war
By one, by two, by three, a.
Well hail'd, well hail'd, you jolly gallants,

[Chair and stools out.

And whither now are you bound a?
O let me have your company till come to the sound a.
There was three fools, fell out about an howlet:
The one sed it was an owl
The other he sed nay,
The third he sed it was a hawk, and her bels were cut away.

3ᴿᴰ COUNTRYMAN
There's a dainty mad woman Mr. comes i'th' Nick, as mad as a march Hare; If we can get her dance, we are made again: I warrant her, she'll do the rarest gambols.

1ˢᵀ COUNTRYMAN
A mad woman? we are made Boys.

SCHOOLMASTER

And are you mad good woman?

DAUGHTER
I would be sorry else,
Give me your hand.

SCHOOLMASTER
Why?

DAUGHTER
I can tell your fortune.
You are a fool: tell ten, I have poz'd him: Buz
Friend you must eat no white bread, if you do
Your teeth will bleed extremely, shall we dance ho?
I know you, y'are a Tinker: Sir, ha Tinker
Stop no more holes, but what you should.

SCHOOLMASTER
Dii boni. A Tinker Damzell?

DAUGHTER
Or a Conjurer: raise me a devill now; and let him play.
Quipassa, o'th' bels and bones.

SCHOOLMASTER
Go take her, and fluently persuade her to a peace:
Et opus exegi, quod nec Jovis ira, nec ignis.
Strike up, and lead her in.

2ND COUNTRYMAN
Come Lass, lets trip it.

DAUGHTER
I'll lead.

[Wind Horns.

3RD COUNTRYMAN
Doe, doe.

SCHOOLMASTER
Persuasively, and cunningly: away boys,

[Exit all but **SCHOOLMASTER**.

I hear the horns: give me some
Meditation, and mark your Cue;
Pallas inspire me.

[Enter **THESEUS, PERITHOUS, HIPPOLITO, EMILIA, ARCITE**: and train.

THESEUS
This way the Stag took.

SCHOOLMASTER
Stay, and edifie.

THESEUS
What have we here?

PERITHOUS
Some Countrey sport, upon my life Sir.

THESEUS
Well Sir, goe forward, we will edifie.
Ladies sit down, we'll stay it.

SCHOOLMASTER
Thou doughtie Duke all hail: all hail sweet Ladies.

THESEUS
This is a cold beginning.

SCHOOLMASTER
If you but favor; our Country pastime made is,
We are a few of those collected here
That ruder Tongues distinguish villager,
And to say veritie, and not to fable;
We are a merry rout, or else a rable
Or company, or by a figure, Chorus
That for thy dignitie will dance a Morris.
And I that am the rectifier of all
By title Pedagogus, that let fall
The Birch upon the breeches of the small ones,
And humble with a Ferula the tall ones,
Doe here present this Machine, or this frame
And daintie Duke, whose doughtie dismall fame
From Dis to Dedalus, from post to pillar
Is blown abroad; help me thy poor well willer,
And with thy twinckling eyes, look right and straight
Upon this mighty Morr—of mickle waight
Is—now comes in, which being glew'd together
Makes Morris, and the cause that we came hither
The body of our sport of no small study
I first appear, though rude, and raw, and muddy,
To speak before thy noble grace, this tenner:

At whose great feet I offer up my penner.
The next the Lord of May, and Lady bright,
The Chambermaid, and Servingman by night
That seek out silent hanging: Then mine Host
And his fat Spouse, that welcomes to their cost
The gauled Traveller, and with a beck'ning
Informes the Tapster to inflame the reck'ning:
Then the beast eating Clown, and next the fool,
The Bavian, with long tail, and eke long tool
Cum multis aliis, that make a dance,
Say I, and all shall presently advance.

THESEUS
I, I by any means, dear Domine.

PERITHOUS
Produce.

[Musick Dance.

Intrate filii, Come forth, and foot it.

[Knock for **SCHOOLMASTER**.

[Enter The Dance.

Ladies, if we have been merry
And have pleas'd thee with a derry,
And a derry, and a down
Say the Schoolmaster's no Clown.
Duke, if we have pleas'd thee too
And have done as good Boys should doe
Give us but a tree or twaine
For a Maypole, and again
Ere another year run out
We'll make thee laugh and all this rout.

THESEUS
Take twenty. Domine; how does my sweet heart?

HIPPOLITO
Never so pleas'd Sir.

EMILIA
'Twas an excellent dance, and for a preface
I never heard a better.

THESEUS

Schoolmaster, I thank you, One see'em all rewarded.

PERITHOUS
And heer's something to paint your Pole withall.

THESEUS
Now to our sports again.

SCHOOLMASTER
May the Stag thou huntst stand long,
And thy dogs be swift and strong:
May they kill him without lets,
And the Ladies eat his dowsets: Come we are all made.

[Wind Horns.

Dii Deæq; Omnes, ye have danc'd rarely wenches.

[Exeunt.

SCÆNA SEXTA

Enter **PALAMON** from the Bush.

PALAMON
About this hour my Cosen gave his faith
To visit me again, and with him bring
Two Swords, and two good Armors; If he fail
He's neither man, nor Soldier; When he left me
I did not think a week could have restor'd
My lost strength to me, I was grown so low,
And Crest-fal'n with my wants: I thank thee Arcite,
Thou art yet a fair Foe; And I feel my self
With this refreshing, able once again
To out-dure danger: To delay it longer
Would make the world think when it comes to hearing,
That I lay fatting like a Swine, to fight
And not a Soldier: Therefore this blest morning
Shall be the last; And that Sword he refuses,
If it but hold, I kill him with; 'tis Justice:
So love, and Fortune for me: O good morrow.

[Enter **ARCITE** with Armors and Swords.

ARCITE
Good morrow noble kinsman.

PALAMON
I have put you
To too much pains Sir.

ARCITE
That too much fair Cosen,
Is but a debt to honor, and my duty.

PALAMON
Would you were so in all Sir; I could wish ye
As kind a kinsman, as you force me find
A beneficiall foe, that my embraces
Might thank ye, not my blows.

ARCITE
I shall think either
Well done, a noble recompence.

PALAMON
Then I shall quit you.

ARCITE
Defy me in these fair terms, and you show
More than a Mistris to me, no more anger
As you love any thing that's honorable:
We were not bred to talk man, when we are arm'd
And both upon our guards, then let our fury
Like meeting of two tides, fly strongly from us,
And then to whom the birthright of this Beauty
Truely pertains (without obbraidings, scorns,
Dispisings of our persons, and such powtings
Fitter for Girles and Schooleboyes) will be seen
And quickly, yours, or mine: Wilt please you arme Sir?
Or if you feel your self not fitting yet
And furnish'd with your old strength, I'll stay Cosen
And ev'ry day discourse you into health,
As I'm spar'd, your person I 'm friends with
And I could wish I had not said I lov'd her
Though I had dide; But loving such a Lady
And justifying my Love, I must not fly from't.

PALAMON
Arcite, thou art so brave an enemy
That no man but thy Cosen's fit to kill thee,
I'm well, and lusty, choose your Armes.

ARCITE

Choose you Sir.

PALAMON
Wilt thou exceed in all, or do'st thou doe it
To make me spare thee?

ARCITE
If you think so Cosen,
You are deceiv'd, for as I 'm a Soldier,
I will not spare you.

PALAMON
That's well said.

ARCITE
You'll find it.

PALAMON
Then as I am an honest man and love,
With all the justice of affection
I'll pay thee soundly: This I'll take.

ARCITE
That's mine then,
I'll arme you first.

PALAMON
Do: Pray thee tell me Cosen,
Where gotst thou this good Armor?

ARCITE
'Tis the Dukes,
And to say true, I stole it, doe I pinch you?

PALAMON
No.

ARCITE
Is't not too heavie?

PALAMON
I have worn a lighter,
But I shall make it serve.

ARCITE
I'll buckl't close.

PALAMON

By any means.

ARCITE
You care not for a Grand guard?

PALAMON
No, no, we'll use no horses, I perceive
You would fain be at that Fight.

ARCITE
I'm indifferent.

PALAMON
Faith so am I: Good Cosen, thrust the buckle
Through far enough.

ARCITE
I warrant you.

PALAMON
My Cask now.

ARCITE
Will you fight bare-arm'd?

PALAMON
We shall be the nimbler.

ARCITE
But use your Gantlets though; those are o'th' least,
Prethee take mine good Cosen.

PALAMON
Thank you Arcite.
How doe I look, am I falen much away?

ARCITE
Faith very little; Love has us'd you kindly.

PALAMON
I'll warrant thee, I'll strike home.

ARCITE
Doe, and spare not;
I'll give you cause sweet Cosen.

PALAMON
Now to you Sir,

Me thinks this Armor's very like that, Arcite,
Thou wor'st that day the 3. Kings fell, but lighter.

ARCITE
That was a very good one, and that day
I well remember, you out-did me Cosen,
I never saw such valour: When you charg'd
Upon the left wing of the Enemie,
I spur'd hard to come up, and under me
I had a right good horse.

PALAMON
You had indeed
A bright Bay I remember.

ARCITE
Yes but all
Was vainly labour'd in me, you out-went me,
Nor could my wishes reach you; Yet a little
I did by imitation.

PALAMON
More by virtue,
You are modest Cosen.

ARCITE
When I saw you charge first,
Me thought I heard a dreadfull clap of Thunder
Break from the Troop.

PALAMON
But still before that flew
The lightning of your valour: Stay a little,
Is not this peece too streight?

ARCITE
No, no, 'tis well.

PALAMON
I would have nothing hurt thee but my Sword,
A bruise would be dishonor.

ARCITE
Now I'm perfect.

PALAMON
Stand off then.

ARCITE
Take my Sword, I hold it better.

PALAMON
I thank ye: No, keep it, your life lyes on it,
Here's one, if it but hold, I aske no more,
For all my hopes: My Cause and honor guard me.

[They bow severall wayes: then advance and stand.

ARCITE
And me my love: Is there ought else to say?

PALAMON
This only, and no more: Thou art mine Aunts Son.
And that blood we desire to shed is mutuall.
In me, thine, and in thee, mine: My Sword
Is in my hand, and if thou killst me
The gods, and I forgive thee; If there be
A place prepar'd for those that sleep in honor,
I wish his wearie soul, that falls may win it:
Fight bravely Cosen, give me thy noble hand.

ARCITE
Here Palamon: This hand shall never more
Come near thee with such friendship.

PALAMON
I commend thee.

ARCITE
If I fall, curse me, and say I was a coward,
For none but such, dare die in these just Tryalls.
Once more farewell my Cosen.

PALAMON
Farewell **ARCITE**

[Fight.

[Horns within: they stand.

ARCITE
Loe Cosen, loe, our Folly has undone us.

PALAMON
Why?

ARCITE
This is the Duke, a hunting as I told you,
If we be found, we're wretched, O retire
For honors sake, and safely presently
Into your Bush agen; Sir we shall find
Too many hours to dye in, gentle Cosen:
If you be seen you perish instantly
For breaking prison, and I, if you reveal me,
For my contempt; Then all the world will scorn us,
And say we had a noble difference,
But base disposers of it.

PALAMON
No, no, Cosen
I will no more be hidden, nor put off
This great adventure to a second Tryall
I know your cunning, and I know your cause,
He that faints now, shame take him, put thy self
Upon thy present guard.

ARCITE
You are not mad?

PALAMON
Or I will make th'advantage of this hour
Mine own, and what to come shall threaten me,
I fear less then my fortune: Know weak Cosen
I love Emilia, and in that I'll bury
Thee, and all crosses else.

ARCITE
Then come, what can come
Thou shalt know Palamon, I dare as well
Die, as discourse, or sleep: Only this fears me,
The law will have the honor of our ends,
Have at thy life.

PALAMON
Look to thine own well **ARCITE**

[Fight again. Horns.

[Enter **THESEUS, HIPPOLITA, EMILIA, PERITHOUS** and train.

THESEUS
What ignorant and mad malicious Traitors,
Are you? That 'gainst the tenor of my Laws

Are making Battail, thus like Knights appointed,
Without my leave, and Officers of Armes?
By Castor both shall dye.

PALAMON
Hold thy word Theseus,
We are certainly both Traitors, both despisers
Of thee, and of thy goodness: I'm Palamon
That cannot love thee, he that broke thy Prison,
Think well, what that deserves; And this is Arcite
A bolder Traytor never trod thy ground,
A Falser never seem'd friend: This is the man
Was beg'd and banish'd, this is he contemnes thee
And what thou dar'st doe; and in this disguise
Against this own Edict follows thy Sister,
That fortunate bright Star, the fair Emilia
Whose servant, (if there be a right in seeing,
And first bequeathing of the soul to) justly
I am, and which is more, dares think her his.
This treacherie like a most trusty Lover,
I call'd him now to answer; If thou be'st
As thou art spoken, great and virtuous,
The true decider of all injuries,
Say, Fight again, and thou shalt see me Theseus
Doe such a Justice, thou thy self wilt envie
Then take my life, I'll wooe thee to't.

PERITHOUS
O Heaven,
What more than man is this!

THESEUS
I have sworn.

ARCITE
We seek not
Thy breath of mercy Theseus, 'Tis to me
A thing as soon to dye, as thee to say it,
And no more mov'd: where this man calls me Traitor,
Let me say thus much; If in love be Treason,
In service of so excellent a Beautie,
As I love most, and in that faith will perish,
As I have brought my life here to confirme it,
As I have serv'd her truest, worthiest,
As I dare kill this Cosen, that denies it,
So let me be most Traitor, and ye please me:
For scorning thy Edict Duke, aske that Lady
Why she is fair, and why her eyes command me

Stay here to love her. And if she say Traytor,
I'm a villain fit to lye unburied.

PALAMON
Thou shalt have pity of us both, O Theseus,
If unto neither thou shew mercy, stop
(As thou art just) thy noble ear against us,
As thou art valiant; For thy Cosens soul
Whose 12. strong labors crown his memory,
Let's die together, at one instant, Duke,
Only a little let him fall before me,
That I may tell my Soul he shall not have her.

THESEUS
I grant your wish, for to say true, your Cosen
Has ten times more offended, for I gave him
More mercy than you found, Sir, your offences
Being no more than his: None here speak for 'em
For ere the Sun set, both shall sleep for ever.

HIPPOLITA
Alas the pity, now or never Sister
Speak not to be denied; That face of yours
Will bear the curses else of after ages
For these lost Cosens.

EMILIA
In my face dear Sister
I find no anger to'em; Nor no ruin,
The misadventure of their own eyes kill'em;
Yet that I will be woman, and have pitty,
My knees shall grow to'th' ground but I'll get mercie.
Help me dear Sister, in a deed so virtuous,
The powers of all women will be with us,
Most royall Brother.

HIPPOLITA
Sir by our tye of Marriage.

EMILIA
By your own spotless honor.

HIPPOLITO
By that faith,
That fair hand, and that honest heart you gave me.

EMILIA
By that you would have pitty in another,

By your own virtues infinite.

HIPPOLITO
By valor,
By all the chast nights I have ever pleas'd you.

THESEUS
These are strange Conjurings.

PERITHOUS
Nay then I'll in too: By all our friendship Sir, by
all our dangers,
By all you love most, wars; And this sweet Lady.

EMILIA
By that you would have trembled to deny
A blushing Maid.

HIPPOLITO
By your own eyes: By strength
In which you swore I went beyond all women,
Almost all men, and yet I yielded Theseus.

PERITHOUS
To crown all this; By your most noble soul
Which cannot want due mercie, I beg first.

HIPPOLITO
Next hear my prayers.

EMILIA
Last let me intreat Sir.

PERITHOUS
For mercy.

HIPPOLITO
Mercy.

EMILIA
Mercy on these Princes.

THESEUS
Ye make my faith reel: Say I felt
Compassion to'em both, how would you place it?

EMILIA
Upon their lives: But with their banishments.

THESEUS

You are a right woman, Sister; You have pitty,
But want the understanding where to use it.
If you desire their lives, invent a way
Safer than banishment: Can these two live
And have the agony of love about 'em,
And not kill one another? Every day
They'ld fight about you; Hourly bring your honor
In publique question with their Swords; Be wise then
And here forget 'em; It concerns your credit,
And my oth equally: I have said they die,
Better they fall byth' Law, than one another.
Bow not my honor.

EMILIA

O my noble Brother,
That oth was rashly made, and in your anger,
Your reason will not hold it, if such vows
Stand for express will, all the world must perish.
Beside, I have another oath, gainst yours
Of more authority, I'm sure more love,
Not made in passion neither, but good heed.

THESEUS

What is it Sister?

PERITHOUS

Urge it home brave Lady.

EMILIA

That you would never deny me any thing
Fit for my modest suit, and your free granting:
I tye you to your word now, if ye fall in't,
Think how you maim your honor;
(For now I'm set a begging Sir, I'm deaf
To all but your compassion) how, their lives
Might breed the ruin of my name; Opinion,
Shall any thing that loves me perish for me?
That were a cruell wisdom, doe men proyn
The straight young Bows that blush with thousand Blossoms
Because they may be rotten? O Duke Theseus
The goodly Mothers that have groan'd for these,
And all the longing Maids that ever lov'd,
If your vow stand, shall curse me and my Beauty,
And in their funerall songs, for these two Cosens
Despise my crueltie, and cry woe worth me,
Till I'm nothing but the scorn of women;

For Heavens sake save their lives, and banish 'em.

THESEUS
On what conditions?

EMILIA
Swear'em never more
To make me their Contention, or to know me,
To tread upon the Dukedome, and to be
Where ever they shall travel, ever strangers to one another.

PALAMON
I'll be cut a peeces
Before I take this oath, forget I love her?
O all ye gods dispise me then: Thy Banishment
I not mislike, so we may fairly carry
Our Swords, and cause along: Else never trifle,
But take our lives Duke, I must love and will,
And for that love, must and dare kill this Cosen
On any peece the earth has.

THESEUS
Will you Arcite
Take these conditions?

PALAMON
He's a villain then.

PERITHOUS
These are men.

ARCITE
No, never Duke: 'Tis worse to me than begging
To take my life so basely, though I think
I never shall enjoy her, yet I'll preserve
The honor of affection, and dye for her,
Make death a Devill.

THESEUS
What may be done? For now I feel compassion.

PERITHOUS
Let it not fall again Sir.

THESEUS
Say Emilia
If one of them were dead, as one must, are you
Content to take th'other to your husband?

They cannot both enjoy you; They are Princes
As goodly as your own eyes, and as noble
As ever fame yet spoke of: Look upon'em,
And if you can love, end this difference,
I give consent, are you content too, Princes?

BOTH
With all our souls.

THESEUS
He that she refuses
Must dye then.

BOTH
Any death thou canst invent Duke.

PALAMON
If I fall from that mouth, I fall with favor.
And Lovers yet unborn shall bless my ashes.

ARCITE
If she refuse me, yet my grave will wed me,
And Soldiers sing my Epitaph.

THESEUS
Make choice then.

EMILIA
I cannot Sir, they are both too excellent
For me, a hayr shall never fall of these men.

HIPPOLITO
What will become of 'em?

THESEUS
Thus I ordain it,
And by mine honor, once again it stands,
Or both shall dye. You shall both to your Countrey,
And each within this month accompanied
With three fair Knights, appear again in this place,
In which I'll plant a Pyramid; And whether
Before us that are here, can force his Cosen
By fair and knightly strength to touch the Pillar,
He shall enjoy her: The other loose his head,
And all his friends: Nor shall he grudge to fall,
Nor think he dies with interest in this Lady:
Will this content ye?

PALAMON
Yes: Here Cosen Arcite
I'm friends again, till that hour.

ARCITE
I embrace ye.

THESEUS
Are you content Sister?

EMILIA
Yes, I must Sir,
Else both miscarry.

THESEUS
Come shake hands again then,
And take heed, as you are Gentlemen, this Quarrell
Sleep till the hour prefixt, and hold your course.

PALAMON
We dare not fail thee Theseus.

THESEUS
Come, I'll give ye
Now usage like to Princes, and to Friends:
When ye return, who wins, I'll settle here,
Who loses, yet I'll weep upon his Beer.

[Exeunt.

ACTUS QUARTUS

SCÆNA PRIMA

Enter **JAILER** and his **FRIEND**.

JAILER
Hear you no more? was nothing said of me
Concerning the escape of Palamon?
Good Sir remember.

1ST FRIEND
Nothing that I heard,
For I came home before the business
Was fully ended: yet I might perceive
E'r I departed, a great likelyhood

Of both their pardons: for Hippolita,
And fair-ey'd Emilia, upon their knees,
Begg'd with such handsome pitty, that the Duke
Methought stood staggering whether he should follow
His rash oath, or the sweet compassion
Of those two Ladies; and to second them,
That truly noble Prince Perithous
Half his own heart, set in too, that I hope
All shall be well: neither heard I one question
Of your name, or his scape.

[Enter **TWO FRIENDS**.

JAILER
Pray Heaven it hold so.

2ND FRIEND
Be of good comfort man; I bring you news
Good news.

JAILER
They are welcome.

2ND FRIEND
Palamon has clear'd you,
And got your pardon, and discover'd
How, and by whose means he scap'd, which was your Daughter's,
Whose pardon is procured too, and the prisoner
Not to be held ungrateful to her goodness,
Has given a sum of money to her Marriage,
A large one I'll assure you.

JAILER
Ye are a good man
And ever bring good news.

1ST FRIEND
How was it ended?

2ND FRIEND
Why, as it should be; they that ne'er begg'd
But they prevail'd, had their suits fairly granted.
The prisoners have their lives.

1ST FRIEND
I knew 't would be so.

2ND FRIEND

But there be new conditions, which you'll hear of
At better time.

JAILER
I hope they are good.

2ND FRIEND
They are honourable,
How good they'll prove, I know not.

[Enter **WOOER**.

1ST FRIEND
'Twill be known.

WOOER
Alas Sir, where's your Daughter?

JAILER
Why do you ask?

WOOER
Oh Sir, when did you see her?

2ND FRIEND
How he looks!

JAILER
This morning.

WOOER
Was she well? was she in health Sir? when did she sleep?

1ST FRIEND
These are strange questions.

JAILER
I do not think she was very well, for now
You make me mind her, but this very day
I ask'd her questions, and she answer'd me
So far from what she was, so childishly,
So sillily, as if she were a fool,
An Innocent, and I was very angry.
But what of her Sir?

WOOER
Nothing but my pity, but you must know it, and as good by me
As by another that less loves her:

JAILER
Well Sir.

1ST FRIEND
Not right?

2ND FRIEND
Not well?—

WOOER
No Sir, not well.
'Tis too true, she is mad.

1ST FRIEND
It cannot be.

WOOER
Believe, you'll find it so.

JAILER
I half suspected
What you told me: the gods comfort her:
Either this was her love to Palamon,
Or fear of my miscarrying on his scape,
Or both.

WOOER
'Tis likely.

JAILER
But why all this haste, Sir?

WOOER
I'll tell you quickly. As I late was angling
In the great Lake that lies behind the Palace,
From the far shore, thick set with Reeds and Sedges.
As patiently I was attending sport,
I heard a voice, a shrill one, and attentive
I gave my ear, when I might well perceive
'Twas one that sung, and by the smallness of it
A Boy or Woman. I then left my angle
To his own skill, came near, but yet perceiv'd not
Who made the sound; the Rushes, and the Reeds
Had so encompast it: I laid me down
And listned to the words she sung, for then
Through a small glade cut by the Fisher-men,
I saw it was your Daughter.

JAILER
Pray goe on Sir?

WOOER
She sung much, but no sence; only I heard her
Repeat this often. Palamon is gone,
Is gone to th' wood to gather Mulberries,
I'll find him out to morrow.

1ST FRIEND
Pretty soul.

WOOER
His shackles will betray him, he'll be taken,
And what shall I do then? I'll bring a beavy,
A hundred black-ey'd Maids that love as I do
With Chaplets on their heads of Daffadillies,
With cherry lips, and cheeks of Damask Roses,
And all we'll dance an Antique 'fore the Duke,
And beg his pardon; then she talk'd of you, Sir;
That you must lose your head to morrow morning
And she must gather Flowers to bury you,
And see the house made handsome, then she sung
Nothing but willow, willow, willow, and between
Ever was, Palamon, fair Palamon,
And Palamon, was a tall young man. The place
Was knee deep where she sate; her careless Tresses,
A wreath of Bull-rush rounded; about her stuck
Thousand fresh Water Flowers of several colours.
That methought she appear'd like the fair Nymph
That feeds the lake with waters, or as Iris
Newly dropt down from heaven; Rings she made
Of Rushes that grew by, and to 'em spoke
The prettiest posies: thus our true love's ty'd,
This you may loose, not me, and many a one:
And then she wept, and sung again, and sigh'd,
And with the same breath smil'd, and kist her hand.

2ND FRIEND
Alas what pity it is?

WOOER
I made in to her,
She saw me, and straight sought the flood, I sav'd her,
And set her safe to land: when presently
She slipt away, and to the City made,
With such a cry, and swiftness, that believe me

She left me far behind her; three, or four,
I saw from far off cross her, one of 'em
I knew to be your brother, where she staid,
And fell, scarce to be got away: I left them with her.

[Enter **BROTHER**, **DAUGHTER**, and **OTHERS**.

And hither came to tell you: Here they are.

DAUGHTER
May you never more enjoy the light, &c.
Is not this a fine Song?

BROTHER
Oh, a very fine one.

DAUGHTER
I can sing twenty more.

BROTHER
I think you can.

DAUGHTER
Yes truly can I, I can sing the Broom,
And Bonny Robbin. Are not you a Tailor?

BROTHER
Yes.

DAUGHTER
Where's my wedding-Gown?

BROTHER
I'll bring it to morrow.

DAUGHTER
Doe, very rarely, I must be abroad else
To call the Maids, and pay the Minstrels
For I must loose my Maiden-head by cock-light
'Twill never thrive else.
Oh fair, oh sweet, &c.

[Sings.

BROTHER
You must ev'n take it patiently.

JAILER

'Tis true.

DAUGHTER
Good ev'n, good men, pray did you ever hear
Of one young Palamon?

JAILER
Yes wench, we know him.

DAUGHTER
Is't not a fine young Gentleman?

JAILER
'Tis Love.

BROTHER
By no mean cross her, she is then distemper'd
For worse than now she shows.

1ST FRIEND
Yes, he's a fine man.

DAUGHTER
Oh, is he so? you have a Sister.

1ST FRIEND
Yes.

DAUGHTER
But she shall never have him, tell her so,
For a trick that I know, y'had best look to her,
For if she see him once, she's gone, she's done,
And undone in an hour. All the young Maids
Of our Town are in love with him, but I laugh at 'em
And let 'em all alone, is't not a wise course?

1ST FRIEND
Yes.

DAUGHTER
There is at least two hundred now with child by him,
There must be four; yet I keep close for all this,
Close as a Cockle; and all these must be boys,
He has the trick on't, and at ten years old
They must be all gelt for Musicians,
And sing the wars of Theseus.

2ND FRIEND

This is strange.

DAUGHTER
As ever you heard, but say nothing.

1ST FRIEND
No.

DAUGHTER
They come from all parts of the Dukedom to him,
I'll warrant ye, he had not so few last night
As twenty, to dispatch, he'll tickle't up
In two hours, if his hand be in.

JAILER
She's lost
Past all cure.

BROTHER
Heaven forbid man.

DAUGHTER
Come hither, you are a wise man.

1ST FRIEND
Does she know him?

2ND FRIEND
No, would she did.

DAUGHTER
You are master of a Ship?

JAILER
Yes.

DAUGHTER
Where's your Compass?

JAILER
Here.

DAUGHTER
Set it to th' North.
And now direct your course to th' wood, where Palamon
Lies longing for me; for the Tackling
Let me alone; come weigh my hearts, cheerly.

ALL
Owgh, owgh, owgh, 'tis up, the wind's fair, top the
Bowling; out with the main sail, where's your
Whistle Master?

BROTHER
Let's get her in.

JAILER
Up to the top Boy.

BROTHER
Where's the Pilot?

1ˢᵀ FRIEND
Here.

DAUGHTER
What ken'st thou?

3ᴿᴰ FRIEND
A fair wood.

DAUGHTER
Bear for it master: tack about:

[Sings.

When Cinthia with her borrowed light, &c.

[Exeunt.

SCÆNA SECUNDA

Enter **EMILIA** alone, with two Pictures.

EMILIA
Yet I may bind those wounds up, that must open
And bleed to death for my sake else; I'll choose,
And end their strife: two such young handsome men
Shall never fall for me, their weeping Mothers,
Following the dead cold ashes of their Sons
Shall never curse my cruelty: Good Heaven;
What a sweet face has Arcite, if wise nature
With all her best endowments, all those beauties
She sowes into the births of noble bodies,

Were here a mortal woman, and had in her
The coy denials of young Maids, yet doubtless,
She would run mad for this man: what an eye!
Of what a fiery sparkle, and quick sweetness:
Has this young Prince! here Love himself sits smiling,
Just such another wanton Ganimead,
Set Love a fire with, and enforc'd the god
Snatch up the goodly Boy, and set him by him
A shining constellation: what a brow,
Of what a spacious Majesty he carries!
Arch'd like the great ey'd Juno's, but far sweeter,
Smoother than Pelops Shoulder! Fame and Honor
Methinks from hence, as from a Promontory
Pointed in heaven, should clap their wings, and sing
To all the under world, the Loves, and Fights
Of gods, and such men near 'em. Palamon,
Is but his foil, to him, a mere dull shadow,
He's swarth, and meagre, of an eye as heavy
As if he had lost his mother; a still temper,
No stirring in him, no alacrity,
Of all this sprightly sharpness, not a smile;
Yet these that we count errors, may become him:
Narcissus was a sad Boy, but a heavenly:
Oh who can find the bent of womans fancy?
I'm a fool, my reason is lost in me,
I have no choice, and I have ly'd so lewdly
That Women ought to beat me. On my knees
I ask thy pardon: Palamon, thou art alone,
And only beautiful, and these the eyes,
These the bright lamps of Beauty that command
And threaten Love, and what young Maid dare cross 'em
What a bold gravity, and yet inviting
Has this brown manly face! Oh Love, this only
From this hour is complexion: lye there Arcite,
Thou art a changling to him, a mere Gipsie.
And this the noble Bodie: I am sotted,
Utterly lost: My Virgins faith has fled me.
For if my Brother, but even now had ask'd me
Whether I lov'd, I had run mad for Arcite.
Now if my Sister; More for Palamon.
Stand both together: now, come ask me Brother,
Alas, I know not: ask me now sweet Sister,
I may go look; what a mere child is Fancie,
That having two fair gawds of equal sweetness,
Cannot distinguish, but must cry for both.

[Enter **GENTLEMAN**.

EMILIA
How now Sir?

GENTLEMAN
From the Noble Duke your Brother
Madam, I bring you news: the Knights are come.

EMILIA
To end the quarrel?

GENTLEMAN
Yes.

EMILIA
Would I might end first:
What sins have I committed, chaste Diana,
That my unspotted youth must now be soil'd
With bloud of Princes? and my Chastity
Be made the Altar, where the Lives of Lovers,
Two greater, and two better never yet
Made Mothers joy, must be the sacrifice
To my unhappy Beauty?

[Enter **THESEUS, HIPPOLITA, PERITHOUS,** and **ATTENDANTS.**

THESEUS
Bring 'em in quickly,
By any means I long to see 'em.
Your two contending Lovers are return'd,
And with them their fair Knights: Now my fair Sister,
You must love one of them.

EMILIA
I had rather both,
So neither for my sake should fall untimely.

[Enter **MESSENGER. CURTIS.**

THESEUS
Who saw 'em?

PERITHOUS
I a while.

GENTLEMAN
And I.

THESEUS

From whence come you, Sir?

MESSENGER
From the Knights.

THESEUS
Pray speak
You that have seen them, what they are.

MESSENGER
I will Sir,
And truly what I think: six braver spirits
Than those they have brought, (if we judge by the outside)
I never saw, nor read of: he that stands
In the first place with Arcite, by his seeming
Should be a stout man, by his face a Prince,
(His very looks so say him) his complexion,
Nearer a brown, than black; stern, and yet noble,
Which shews him hardy, fearless, proud of dangers:
The circles of his eyes, shew fair within him,
And as a heated Lion, so he looks:
His hair hangs long behind him, black and shining
Like Ravens wings: his shoulders broad, and strong,
Arm'd long and round, and on his Thigh a Sword
Hung by a curious Bauldrick: when he frowns
To seal his Will with, better o' my conscience
Was never Soldiers friend.

THESEUS
Thou hast well describ'd him.

PERITHOUS
Yet, a great deal short
Methinks, of him that's first with Palamon.

THESEUS
Pray speak him friend.

PERITHOUS
I ghess he is a Prince too,
And if it may be, greater; for his show
Has all the ornament of honor in't:
He's somewhat bigger than the Knight he spoke of,
But of a face far sweeter; his complexion
Is (as a ripe Grape) ruddy: he has felt
Without doubt, what he fights for, and so apter
To make this cause his own: in's face appears
All the fair hopes of what he undertakes,

And when he's angry, then a setled valour
(Not tainted with extreams) runs through his body,
And guides his arm to brave things: Fear he cannot,
He shews no such soft temper, his head's yellow,
Hard hair'd, and curl'd, thick twin'd, like Ivy tops,
Not to undoe with thunder; in his face
The Livery of the warlike Maid appears,
Pure red and white, for yet no beard has blest him.
And in his rowling eyes sits victory,
As if she ever meant to correct his valour:
His Nose stands high, a Character of honor,
His red Lips, after fights, are fit for Ladies.

EMILIA
Must these men die too?

PERITHOUS
When he speaks, his tongue
Sounds like a Trumpet; all his lineaments
Are as a man would wish 'em, strong and clean,
He wears a well-steel'd Axe, the staffe of Gold,
His age some five and twenty.

MESSENGER
There's another,
A little man, but of a tough soul, seeming
As great as any, fairer promises
In such a Body yet I never look'd on.

PERITHOUS
Oh he that's freckle fac'd?

MESSENGER
The same my Lord,
Are they not sweet ones?

PERITHOUS
Yes, they are well.

MESSENGER
Methinks,
Being so few, and well dispos'd, they shew
Great, and fine Art in nature, he's white hair'd,
Not wanton white, but such a manly colour
Next to an aborn, tough, and nimble set,
Which shows an active soul: his arms are brawny
Lin'd with strong sinews: to the shoulder-piece,
Gently they swell, like Women new conceiv'd,

Which speaks him prone to labour, never fainting
Under the weight of Arms, stout-hearted still,
But when he stirs, a Tiger; he's grey ey'd,
Which yields compassion where he conquers: sharp
To spie advantages, and where he finds 'em,
He's swift to make 'em his: He does no wrongs,
Nor takes none; he's round fac'd, and when he smiles
He shows a Lover, when he frowns, a Soldier:
About his head he wears the winners oak,
And in it stuck the favour of his Lady:
His age, some six and thirty. In his hand
He bears a Charging Staffe, emboss'd with Silver.

THESEUS
Are they all thus?

PERITHOUS
They are all the sons of honor.

THESEUS
Now as I have a soul, I long to see 'em,
Lady, you shall see men fight now.

HIPPOLITO
I wish it,
But not the cause my Lord; They would shew
Bravely about the Titles of two Kingdoms;
'Tis pity Love should be so tyrannous:
Oh my soft-hearted Sister, what think you?
Weep not, till they weep bloud: Wench it must be.

THESEUS
You have steel'd 'em with your Beauty: honor'd friend,
To you I give the Field; pray order it,
Fitting the persons that must use it.

PERITHOUS
Yes Sir.

THESEUS
Come, I'll go visit 'em: I cannot stay,
Their fame has fir'd me so; till they appear,
Good friend be royal.

PERITHOUS
There shall want no bravery.

EMILIA

Poor wench go weep, for whosoever wins,
Looses a noble Cosin, for thy sins.

[Exeunt.

Enter **JAILER, WOOER, DOCTOR**.

DOCTOR
Her distraction is more at some time of the Moon,
Than at other some, is it not?

JAILER
She is continually in a harmless distemper, sleeps
Little, altogether without appetite, save often drinking,
Dreaming of another world, and a better; and what
Broken piece of matter so e'er she's about, the name
Palamon lards it, that she farces ev'ry business

[Enter **DAUGHTER**.

Withal, fits it to every question; Look where
She comes, you shall perceive her behaviour.

DAUGHTER
I have forgot it quite; the burden on't was Down
A down a: and penn'd by no worse man, than
Giraldo, Emilias Schoolmaster; he's as
Fantastical too, as ever he may goe upon's legs,
For in the next world will Dido see Palamon, and
Then will she be out of love with Æneas.

DOCTOR
What stuff's here? poor soul.

JAILER
Ev'n thus all day long.

DAUGHTER
Now for this Charm, that I told you of, you must
Bring a piece of silver on the tip of your tongue,
Or no ferry: then if it be your chance to come where
The blessed spirits, as there's a sight now; we Maids
That have our Livers, perish, crackt to pieces with
Love, we shall come there, and do nothing all day long

But pick Flowers with Proserpine, then will I make
Palamon a Nosegay, then let him mark me,—then.

DOCTOR
How prettily she's amiss! note her a little farther.

DAUGHTER
Faith I'll tell you, sometime we goe to Barly-break,
We of the blessed; alas, 'tis a sore life they have i' th'
Other place, such burning, frying, boiling, hissing,
Howling, chatt'ring, cursing, oh they have shrowd
Measure, take heed; if one be mad, or hang, or
Drown themselves, thither they goe, Jupiter bless
Us, and there shall we be put in a Cauldron of
Lead, and Usurers grease, amongst a whole million of
Cut-purses, and there boil like a Gamon of Bacon
That will never be enough.

DOCTOR
How her brain coins!

DAUGHTER
Lords and Courtiers, that have got Maids with child,
they are in this place, they shall stand in fire up to the
Navel, and in Ice up to th' heart, and there th' offending part
burns, and the deceiving part freezes; in troth a very grievous
punishment, as one would think, for such a Trifle, believe me
one would marry a leprous witch, to be rid on't I'll assure you.

DOCTOR
How she continues this fancie! 'Tis not an engraffed
madness but a most thick, and profound melancholly.

DAUGHTER
To hear there a proud Lady, and a proud City wife,
howl together: I were a beast, and Il'd call it good sport: one
cries, oh this smoak, another this fire; one cries oh that I
ever did it behind the Arras, and then howls; th' other curses
a suing fellow and her Garden-house.

[Sings
I will be true, my Stars, my Fate, &c.

[Exit **DAUGHTER**.

JAILER
What think you of her, Sir?

DOCTOR
I think she has a perturbed mind, which I cannot
minister to.

JAILER
Alas, what then?

DOCTOR
Understand you, she ever affected any man, e'r
She beheld Palamon?

JAILER
I was once, Sir, in great hope she had fix'd her
Liking on this Gentleman my friend.

WOOER
I did think so too, and would account I had a great
Pen'worth on't, to give half my state, that both
She and I at this present stood unfainedly on the
Same terms.

DOCTOR
That intemperate surfet of her eye, hath distemper'd the
Other sences, they may return and settle again to
Execute their preordained faculties, but they are
Now in a most extravagant vagary. This you
Must doe, confine her to a place, where the light
May rather seem to steal in, than be permitted; take
Upon you (young Sir, her friend) the name of
Palamon; say you come to eat with her, and to
Commune of Love; this will catch her attention, for
This her mind beats upon; other objects that are
Inserted 'tween her mind and eye, become the pranks
And friskins of her madness; sing to her such green
Songs of Love, as she says Palamon hath sung in
Prison; Come to her, stuck in as sweet Flowers as the
Season is mistriss of, and thereto make an addition of
Some other compounded odors, which are grateful to the
Sense: all this shall become Palamon, for Palamon can
Sing, and Palamon is sweet, and ev'ry good thing, desire
To eat with her, carve her, drink to her, and still
Among, intermingle your petition of grace and acceptance
Into her favour: learn what Maids have been her
Companions, and Play-pheers; and let them repair to
Her with Palamon in their mouths, and appear with
Tokens, as if they suggested for him, it is a falshood
She is in, which is with falshoods to be combated.
This may bring her to eat, to sleep, and reduce what's

Now out of square in her, into their former Law, and
Regiment; I have seen it approved, how many times
I know not, but to make the number more, I have
Great hope in this. I will between the passages of
This project, come in with my applyance: Let us
Put it in execution; and hasten the success, which doubt not
Will bring forth comfort.

[Flourish. Exeunt.

ACTUS QUINTUS

SCÆNA PRIMA

Enter **THESEUS, PERITHOUS, HIPPOLITA, ATTENDANTS.**

THESEUS
Now let 'em enter, and before the gods
Tender their holy Prayers: Let the Temples
Burn bright with sacred fires, and the Altars
In hallowed clouds commend their swelling Incense
To those above us: Let no due be wanting,

[Flourish of Cornets.

They have a noble work in hand, will honor
The very powers that love 'em.

[Enter **PALAMON** and **ARCITE**, and their **KNIGHTS**.

PERITHOUS
Sir, they enter.

THESEUS
You valiant and strong-hearted enemies
You royal German foes, that this day come
To blow that nearness out, that flames between ye;
Lay by your anger for an hour, and Dove-like
Before the holy Altars of your helpers
(The all-fear'd gods) bow down your stubborn bodies,
Your Ire is more than mortal; So your help be,
And as the gods regard ye, fight with Justice,
I'll leave you to your prayers, and betwixt ye
I part my wishes.

PERITHOUS

Honor crown the worthiest.

[Exit **THESEUS** and his train.

PALAMON
The glass is running now that cannot finish
Till one of us expire: think you but thus,
That were there ought in me which strove to shew
Mine enemy in this business, were't one eye
Against another: Arm opprest by Arm:
I would destroy th' offender, Coz. I would
Though parcel of my self: then from this gather
How I should tender you.

ARCITE
I am in labour
To push your name, your antient love, our kindred
Out of my memory; and i' th' self-same place
To seat something I would confound: so hoist we
The sails, that must these vessels port, even where
The heavenly Lymiter pleases.

PALAMON
You speak well;
Before I turn, let me embrace thee Cosin
This I shall never do agen.

ARCITE
One farewel.

PALAMON
Why let it be so: Farewel Coz.

[Exeunt **PALAMON** and his **KNIGHTS**.

ARCITE
Farewel Sir;
Knights, Kinsmen, Lovers, yea my Sacrifices
True worshipers of Mars, whose spirit in you
Expells the seeds of fear, and th' apprehension
Which still is farther off it, goe with me
Before the god of our profession: There
Require of him the hearts of Lions, and
The breath of Tygers, yea, the fierceness too,
Yea, the speed also, to go on, I mean
Else wish we to be snails: you know my prize
Must be dragg'd out of bloud, force and great feate
Must put my Garland on, where she sticks

The Queen of Flowers: our intercession then
Must be to him that makes the Camp, a Cestron
Brim'd with the blood of men: give me your aid
And bend your spirits towards him.

[They kneel.

Thou mighty one, that with thy power hast turn'd
Green Neptune into purple.
Comets prewarn, whose havock in vast Field
Unearthed skulls proclaim, whose breath blows down,
The teeming Ceres foyzon, who dost pluck
With hand armenipotent from forth blew clouds,
The mason'd Turrets, that both mak'st and break'st
The stony girths of Cities: me thy pupil,
Youngest follower of thy Drum, instruct this day
With military skill, that to thy laud
I may advance my streamer, and by thee,
Be stil'd the Lord o' th' day, give me great Mars
Some token of thy Pleasure.

[Here they fall on their faces as formerly, and there is heard clanging of Armor, with a short Thunder, as the burst of a battel, whereupon they all rise, and bow to the Altar.

Oh great Corrector of enormous times,
Shaker of o'er-rank States, thou grand decider
Of dusty, and old Titles, that heal'st with blood
The earth when it is sick, and curst the world
O' th' pluresie of people; I do take
Thy signs auspiciously, and in thy name
To my design; march boldly, let us goe.

[Exeunt.

[Enter **PALAMON** and his **KNIGHTS**, with the former observance.

PALAMON
Our stars must glister with new fire, or be
To day extinct; our argument is love,
Which if the goddess of it grant, she gives
Victory too, then blend your spirits with mine,
You, whose free nobleness do make my cause
Your personal hazard; to the goddess Venus
Commend we our proceeding, and implore
Her power unto our partie.

[Here they kneel as formerly.

Hail Sovereign Queen of secrets, who hast power
To call the fiercest Tyrant from his rage;
And weep unto a Girl; that hast the might
Even with an eye-glance, to choak Marsis Drum
And turn th' allarm to whispers, that canst make
A Cripple florish with his Crutch, and cure him
Before Apollo; that may'st force the King
To be his subjects vassal, and induce
Stale gravity to daunce, the pould Batchelor
Whose youth like wanton boys through Bonfires
Have skipt thy flame, at seventy, thou canst catch
And make him to the scorn of his hoarse throat
Abuse young lays of Love; what godlike power
Hast thou not power upon? To Phoebus thou
Add'st flames, hotter than his the heavenly fires
Did scorch his mortal Son, thine him; the huntress
All moist and cold, some say, began to throw
Her Bow away, and sigh: take to thy grace
Me thy vow'd Soldier, who do bear thy yoak
As 'twere a wreath of Roses, yet is heavier
Than Lead it self, stings more than Nettles;
I have never been foul-mouth'd against thy Law,
Ne'er reveal'd secret, for I knew none; would not
Had I ken'd all that were; I never practis'd
Upon mans wife, nor would the Libels read
Of liberal wits: I never at great feasts
Sought to betray a beauty, but have blush'd
At simpring Sirs that did: I have been harsh
To large Confessors, and have hotly ask'd 'em
If they had Mothers, I had one, a woman,
And women 't were they wrong'd. I knew a man
Of eighty winters, this I told them, who
A Lass of fourteen brided, 'twas thy power
To put life into dust, the aged Cramp
Had screw'd his square foot round,
The Gout had knit his fingers into knots,
Torturing Convulsions from his globy eies,
Had almost drawn their spheres, that what was life
In him seem'd torture: this Anatomie
Had by his young fair pheare a Boy, and I
Believ'd it was his, for she swore it was,
And who would not believe her? brief I am
To those that prate, and have done, no Companion;
To those that boast and have not, a defyer;
To those that would and cannot, a Rejoycer.
Yea him I do not love, that tells close offices
The foulest way, nor names concealments in
The boldest language, such a one I am,

And vow that lover never yet made sigh
Truer than I. Oh then most soft sweet goddess
Give me the victory of this question, which
Is true loves merit, and bless me with a sign
Of thy great pleasure.

[Here Musick is heard, Doves are seen to flutter, they fall again upon their faces, then on their knees.

PALAMON
Oh thou that from eleven to ninety reign'st
In mortal bosoms, whose Chase is this world
And we in Herds thy Game; I give thee thanks
For this fair Token, which being laid unto
Mine innocent true heart, arms in assurance

[They bow.

My body to this business; Let us rise
And bow before the goddess: Time comes on.

[Exeunt. Still Musick of Records.

[Enter **EMILIA** in white, her hair about her shoulders, a wheaten wreath: One in white, holding up her train, her hair stuck with Flowers: One before her carrying a silver Hynd, in which is conveyed Incense and sweet odors, which being set upon the Altar, her **MAIDS** standing aloof, she sets fire to it, then they curt'sy and kneel.

EMILIA
Oh sacred, shadowy, cold and constant Queen,
Abandoner of Revels, mute contemplative,
Sweet, solitary, white as chaste, and pure
As wind-fan'd Snow, who to thy femal Knights
Allow'st no more blood than will make a blush,
Which is their Orders Robe. I here thy Priest
Am humbled for thine Altar, oh vouchsafe
With that thy rare green eye, which never yet
Beheld thing maculate, look on thy Virgin,
And sacred silver Mistriss, lend thine ear
(Which ne'r heard scurril term, into whose port
Ne'er entred wanton sound,) to my petition
Season'd with holy fear; this is my last
Of vestal office, I'm Bride-habited,
But Maiden-hearted: a Husband I have pointed,
But do not know him, out of two, I should
Choose one, and pray for his success, but I
Am guiltless of election of mine eyes,
Were I to lose one, they are equal precious,
I could doome neither, that which perish'd should

Goe to't unsentenc'd: Therefore most modest Queen,
He of the two Pretenders, that best loves me
And has the truest Title in't, let him
Take off my wheaten Garland, or else grant
The file and quality I hold, I may
Continue in thy Band.

[Here the Hind vanishes under the Altar: and in the place ascends a Rose-Tree, having one Rose upon it.

See what our General of Ebbs and Flows
Out from the bowels of her holy Altar
With sacred Act advances: But one Rose,
If well inspir'd, this Battel shall confound
Both these brave Knights, and I a Virgin Flower
Must grow alone unpluck'd.

[Here is heard a sodain twang of Instruments, and the Rose falls from the Tree.

The Flower is fall'n, the Tree descends: oh Mistriss
Thou here dischargest me, I shall be gather'd,
I think so, but I know not thine own Will;
Unclaspe thy Mistery: I hope she's pleas'd,
Her Signs were gracious.

[They curt'sey, and Exeunt.

SCÆNA SECUNDA

Enter **DOCTOR**, **JAILER**, and **WOOER**, in habit of Palamon.

DOCTOR
Has this advice I told you, done any good upon her?

WOOER
Oh very much; the Maids that kept her company
Have half perswaded her that I am Palamon; within this
Half hour she came smiling to me, and ask'd me what I
Would eat, and when I would kiss her: I told her,
Presently, and kist her twice.

DOCTOR
'Twas well done; twenty times had been far better,
For there the cure lies mainly.

WOOER
Then she told me

She would watch with me to night, for well she knew
What hour my fit would take me.

DOCTOR
Let her do so,
And when your fit comes, fit her home,
And presently.

WOOER
She would have me sing.

DOCTOR
You did so?

WOOER
No.

DOCTOR
'Twas very ill done then,
You should observe her ev'ry way.

WOOER
Alas
I have no voice Sir, to confirm her that way.

DOCTOR
That's all one, if ye make a noise,
If she intreat again, do any thing,
Lie with her if she ask you.

JAILER
Hoa there Doctor.

DOCTOR
Yes, in the way of cure.

JAILER
But first, by your leave
I' th' way of honesty.

DOCTOR
That's but a niceness,
Nev'r cast your child away for honesty;
Cure her first this way, then if she will be honest,
She has the path before her.

JAILER
Thank ye Doctor.

DOCTOR
Pray bring her in
And let's see how she is.

JAILER
I will, and tell her
Her Palamon staies for her: but Doctor,
Methinks you are i' th' wrong still.

[Exit **JAILER**.

DOCTOR
Goe, goe: you Fathers are fine fools: her honesty?
And we should give her physick till we find that:

WOOER
Why, do you think she is not honest, Sir?

DOCTOR
How old is she?

WOOER
She's eighteen.

DOCTOR
She may be,
But that's all one, 'tis nothing to our purpose,
What ev'r her Father saies, if you perceive
Her Mood inclining that way that I spoke of
Videlicet, The way of flesh, you have me.

WOOER
Yes very well Sir.

DOCTOR
Please her appetite
And do it home, it cures her ipso facto,
The melancholly humor that infects her.

WOOER
I am of your mind, Doctor.

[Enter **JAILER, DAUGHTER, MAID**.

DOCTOR
You'll find it so; she comes, pray honor her.

JAILER
Come, your Love Palamon stays for you child,
And has done this long hour, to visit you.

DAUGHTER
I thank him for his gentle patience,
He's a kind Gentleman, and I am much bound to him,
Did you never see the horse he gave me?

JAILER
Yes.

DAUGHTER
How do you like him?

JAILER
He's a very fair one.

DAUGHTER
You never saw him dance?

JAILER
No.

DAUGHTER
I have often,
He dances very finely, very comely,
And for a Jigg, come cut and long tail to him,
He turns ye like a Top.

JAILER
That's fine indeed.

DAUGHTER
He'll dance the Morris twenty mile an hour.
And that will founder the best hobby-horse
(If I have any skill) in all the parish,
And gallops to the turn of Light a'love,
What think you of this horse?

JAILER
Having these virtues
I think he might be brought to play at Tennis.

DAUGHTER
Alas that's nothing.

JAILER

Can he write and read too?

DAUGHTER
A very fair hand, and casts himself th' accounts
Of all his Hay and Provender: that Hostler
Must rise betime that cozens him; you know
The Chesnut Mare the Duke has?

JAILER
Very well.

DAUGHTER
She is horribly in love with him, poor beast,
But he is like his Master, coy and scornful.

JAILER
What Dowry has she?

DAUGHTER
Some two hundred Bottles,
And twenty strike of Oats; but he'll ne'er have her;
He lisps, in's neighing, able to entice
A Millers Mare,
He'll be the death of her.

DOCTOR
What stuff she utters!

JAILER
Make curt'sie, here your love comes.

WOOER
Pretty soul
How doe ye? that's a fine Maid, there's a curt'sie.

DAUGHTER
Yours to command i'th' way of honesty;
How far is't now to th' end o'th' world my Masters?

DOCTOR
Why a days journey wench.

DAUGHTER
Will you go with me?

WOOER
What shall we do there wench?

DAUGHTER
Why play at Stool-ball.
What is there else to do?

WOOER
I am content
If we shall keep our wedding there.

DAUGHTER
'Tis true
For there I will assure you, we shall find
Some blind Priest for the purpose, that will venture
To marry us, for here they are nice and foolish;
Besides, my Father must be hang'd to morrow
And that would be a blot i'th' business.
Are not you Palamon?

WOOER
Do not you know me?

DAUGHTER
Yes, but you care not for me; I have nothing
But this poor Petticoat, and two course Smocks.

WOOER
That's all one, I will have you.

DAUGHTER
Will you surely?

WOOER
Yes, by this fair hand will I.

DAUGHTER
We'll to bed then.

WOOER
Ev'n when you will.

DAUGHTER
Oh Sir, you would fain be nibling.

WOOER
Why do you rub my kiss off?

DAUGHTER
'Tis a sweet one,
And will perfume me finely against the wedding.

Is not this your Cosin Arcite?

DOCTOR
Yes Sweet heart,
And I am glad my Cosin Palamon
Has made so fair a choice.

DAUGHTER
Do you think he'll have me?

DOCTOR
Yes without doubt.

DAUGHTER
Do you think so too?

JAILER
Yes.

DAUGHTER
We shall have many children: Lord, how y'are growne
My Palamon I hope will grow too finely
Now he's at liberty: alas poor Chicken,
He was kept down with hard Meat, and ill Lodging,
But I'll kiss him up again.

[Enter a **MESSENGER**.

MESSENGER
What do you here? you'll lose the noblest sight,
That e'er was seene.

JAILER
Are they i'th' field?

MESSENGER
They are
You bear a charge there too.

JAILER
I'll away straight
I must ev'n leave you here.

DOCTOR
Nay, we'll goe with you,
I will not loose the Fight.

JAILER

How did you like her?

DOCTOR
I'll warrant you within these three or four days
I'll make her right again. You must not from her
But still preserve her in this way.

WOOER
I will.

DOCTOR
Let's get her in.

WOOER
Come Sweet, we'll go to dinner
And then we'll play at Cards.

DAUGHTER
And shall we kiss too?

WOOER
A hundred times.

DAUGHTER
And twenty.

WOOER
I, and twenty.

DAUGHTER
And then we'll sleep together.

DOCTOR
Take her offer.

WOOER
Yes marry will we.

DAUGHTER
But you shall not hurt me.

WOOER
I will not Sweet.

DAUGHTER
If you do (Love) I'll cry.

[Flourish Exeunt.

SCÆNA TERTIA

Enter **THESEUS, HIPPOLITA, EMILIA, PERITHOUS**: and some **ATTENDANTS, T. TUCK: CURTIS.**

EMILIA
I'll no step further.

PERITHOUS
Will you loose this sight?

EMILIA
I had rather see a Wren hawk at a Fly
Than this decision; ev'ry blow that falls
Threats a brave life, each stroke laments
The place wheron it falls, and sounds more like
A Bell, than Blade, I will stay here,
It is enough, my hearing shall be punish'd,
With what shall happen, 'gainst the which there is
No deafing, but to hear; not taint mine eye
With dread sights, it may shun.

PERITHOUS
Sir, my good Lord
Your Sister will no further.

THESEUS
Oh she must.
She shall see deeds of Honor in their kind,
Which sometime shew well pencill'd. Nature now
Shall make, and act the Story, the belief
Both seal'd with eye, and ear; you must be present,
You are the victors meed, the price, and garland
To crown the Questions Title.

EMILIA
Pardon me,
If I were there, I'd wink.

THESEUS
You must be there;
This trial is as 'twere i' th' night, and you
The only Star to shine.

EMILIA
I am extinct,

There is but envy in that light, which shows
The one the other: darkness which ever was
The dam of horror; who does stand accurst
Of many mortal Millions, may even now
By casting her black mantle over both
That neither could find other, get her self
Some part of a good name, and many a murther
Set off whereto she's guilty.

HIPPOLITO
You must go.

EMILIA
In faith I will not.

THESEUS
Why the Knights must kindle
Their valour at your eye: know of this war
You are the Treasure, and must needs be by
To give the Service pay.

EMILIA
Sir, pardon me,
The Title of a Kingdom may be try'd
Out of it self.

THESEUS
Well, well then, at your pleasure,
Those that remain with you, could wish their office
To any of their enemies.

HIPPOLITO
Farewel Sister,
I am like to know your Husband 'fore your self
By some small start of time, he whom the gods
Doe of the two, know best, I pray them, he
Be made your Lot.

[Exeunt **THESEUS**, **HIPPOLITA**, **PERITHOUS**, &c.

EMILIA
Arcite is gently visag'd; yet his eye
Is like an Engine bent, or a sharp weapon
In a soft sheath; mercy, and manly courage
Are bedfellows in his visage: Palamon
Has a most menacing aspect, his brow
Is grav'd, and seems to bury what it frowns on,
Yet sometimes 'tis not so, but alters to

The quality of his thoughts; long time his eye
Will dwell upon his object. Melancholly
Becomes him nobly; so does Arcite's mirth,
But Palamon's sadness is a kind of mirth,
So mingled, as if mirth did make him sad.
And sadness, merry; those darker humors that
Stick mis-becomingly on others, on them
Live in fair dwelling.

[Cornets. Trumpets sound as to a Charge.

Hark how yon spurs to spirit doe incite
The Princes to their proof, Arcite may win me,
And yet may Palamon wound Arcite, to
The spoiling of his figure. Oh what pity
Enough for such a chance; if I were by
I might do hurt, for they would glance their eies
Toward my Seat, and in that motion might
Omit a Ward, or forfeit an offence
Which crav'd that very time: it is much better

[Cornets. A great cry, and noise within, crying a Palamon.

I am not there, oh better never born
Than minister to such harm, what is the chance?

[Enter SERVANT.

SERVANT
The cry's a Palamon.

EMILIA
Then he has won: 'twas ever likely,
He look'd all grace and success, and he is
Doubtless the prim'st of men: I prethee run
And tell me how it goes.

[Shout, and Cornets: crying a Palamon.

SERVANT
Still Palamon.

EMILIA
Run and enquire, poor Servant thou hast lost,
Upon my right side still I wore thy Picture,
Palamon's on the left, why so I know not,
I had no end in't; else chance would have it so.

[Another cry and shout within, and Cornets.

On the sinister side the heart lies; Palamon
Had the best boding chance: this burst of clamor
Is sure th' end o'th' combat.

[Enter **SERVANT**.

SERVANT
They said that Palamon had Arcites body
Within an inch o'th' Pyramid, that the cry
Was general a Palamon: but anon,
Th' Assistants made a brave redemption, and
The two bold Tytlers, at this instant are
Hand to hand at it.

EMILIA
Were they metamorphos'd
Both into one; oh why? there were no woman
Worth so compos'd a man: their single share,
Their noblenes peculier to them, gives
The prejudice of disparity values shortness

[Cornets. Cry within, Arcite, Arcite.

To any Lady breathing—More exulting?
Palamon still?

SERVANT
Nay, now the sound is Arcite.

EMILIA
I prethee lay attention to the Cry.

[Cornets. A great shout, and cry, Arcite, victory.

Set both thine ears to th' business.

SERVANT
The cry is
Arcite, and victory, hark Arcite, victory,
The Combats consummation is proclaim'd
By the wind Instruments.

EMILIA
Half sights saw
That Arcite was no babe, god's lyd, his richness
And costliness of spirit lookt through him; it could

No more be hid in him, than fire in flax,
Than humble banks can go to law with waters,
That drift winds, force to raging: I did think
Good Palamon would miscarry, yet I knew not
Why I did think so; Our reasons are not prophets
When oft our fancies are: they are coming off:
Alas poor Palamon.

[Cornets.

[Enter **THESEUS**, **HIPPOLITA**, **PERITHOUS**, **ARCITE** as Victor and **ATTENDANTS**, &c.

THESEUS
Lo, where our Sister is in expectation,
Yet quaking, and unsetled: fairest Emilia,
The gods by their Divine arbitrament
Have given you this Knight, he is a good one
As ever struck at head: Give me your hands;
Receive you her, you him, be plighted with
A love that grows, as you decay.

ARCITE
Emily.
To buy you I have lost what's dearest to me,
Save what is bought, and yet I purchase cheaply,
As I do rate your value.

THESEUS
Oh loved Sister,
He speaks now of as brave a Knight as e'er
Did spur a noble Steed: surely the gods
Would have him die a batchelor, lest his race
Should show i'th' world too godlike: his behaviour
So charm'd me, that methought Alcides was
To him a Sow of Lead: if I could praise
Each part of him to th' all I have spoke, your Arcite
Did not lose by't; for he that was thus good
Encountred yet his Better, I have heard
Two emulous Philomels, beat the ear o'th' night
With their contentious throats, now one the higher,
Anon the other, then again the first,
And by and by out-breasted, that the sense
Could not be judge between 'em: so it far'd
Good space between these kinsmen; till heavens did
Make hardly one the winner: wear the Garland
With joy that you have won: for the subdu'd,
Give them our present Justice, since I know
Their lives but pinch 'em, let it here be done:

The Scene's not for our seeing, goe we hence,
Right joyful, with some sorrow. Arm your prize,
I know you will not lose her: Hippolita
I see one eye of yours conceives a tear
The which it will deliver.

[Flourish.

EMILIA
Is this winning?
Oh all you heavenly powers, where is your mercy?
But that your wills have said it must be so,
And charge me live to comfort this unfriended,
This miserable Prince that cuts away
A life more worthy from him, than all women;
I should, and would die too.

HIPPOLITO
Infinite pity
That four such eyes should be so fix'd on one
That two must needs be blind for't.

THESEUS
So it is.

[Exeunt.

SCÆNA QUARTA

Enter **PALAMON** and his **KNIGHTS** pinion'd: **JAILER**, **EXECUTIONER**, &c. **GUARD**.

PALAMON
There's many a man alive that hath out-liv'd
The love o' th' people, yea, i'th' self-same state
Stands many a Father with his child; some comfort
We have by so considering: we expire
And not without mens pity. To live still,
Have their good wishes, we prevent
The lothsome misery of age, beguile
The Gout and Rheum, that in lag hours attend
For grey approachers; we come towards the gods
Young, and unwapper'd, not halting under Crimes
Many and stale: that sure shall please the gods
Sooner than such, to give us Nectar with 'em,
For we are more clear Spirits. My dear kinsmen.
Whose lives (for this poor comfort) are laid down,

You have sold 'em too too cheap.

1ˢᵀ KNIGHT
What ending could be
Of more content? o'er us the victors have
Fortune, whose Title is as momentary,
As to us death is certain: a grain of honor
They not o'er-weigh us.

2ᴺᴰ KNIGHT
Let us bid farewel;
And, with our patience, anger tott'ring Fortune,
Who at her certain'st reels.

3ᴿᴰ KNIGHT
Come: who begins?

PALAMON
Ev'n he that led you to this Banquet, shall
Taste to you all: ah ha my Friend, my Friend,
Your gentle daughter gave me freedom once;
You'll see't done now for ever: pray how does she?
I heard she was not well; her kind of ill
Gave me some sorrow.

JAILER
Sir, she's well restor'd,
And to be married shortly.

PALAMON
By my short life
I am most glad on't; 'tis the latest thing
I shall be glad of, prethee tell her so:
Commend me to her, and to piece her portion
Tender her this.

1ˢᵀ KNIGHT
Nay, let's be offerers all.

2ᴺᴰ KNIGHT
Is it a maid?

PALAMON
Verily I think so,
A right good creature, more to me deserving
Than I can quight or speak of.

ALL KNIGHTS

Commend us to her.

[They give their purses.

JAILER
The gods requite you all,
And make her thankful.

PALAMON
Adieu; and let my life be now as short,
As my leave taking.

[Lies on the Block.

1ST KNIGHT
Lead courageous Cosin.

1ST & 2ND KNIGHTS
We'll follow cheerfully.

[A great noise within, crying, run, save, hold.

[Enter in haste a **MESSENGER**.

MESSENGER
Hold, hold, oh hold, hold, hold.

[Enter **PERITHOUS** in haste.

PERITHOUS
Hold, hoa: It is a cursed haste you made
If you have done so quickly: noble Palamon,
The gods will shew their glory in a life
That thou art yet to lead.

PALAMON
Can that be,
When Venus I have said is false? How do things fare?

PERITHOUS
Arise great Sir, and give the tidings ear
That are most early sweet, and bitter.

PALAMON
What
Hath wak't us from our dream?

PERITHOUS

List then: your Cosin
Mounted upon a Steed that Emily
Did first bestow on him, a black one, owing
Not a hayr worth of white, which some will say
Weakens his price, and many will not buy
His goodness with this note: Which superstition
Hear finds allowance: On this horse is Arcite
Trotting the stones of Athens, which the Calkins
Did rather tell, than trample; For the horse
Would make his length a mile, if't pleas'd his Rider
To put pride in him: as he thus went counting
The flinty pavement, dancing as t'were to'th' Musick
His own hoofs made; (For as they say from iron
Came Musicks origen) what envious Flint,
Cold as old Saturne, and like him possest
With fire malevolent, darted a Spark,
Or what feirce sulphur else, to this end made,
I comment not; The hot horse, hot as fire,
Took Toy at this, and fell to what disorder
His power could give his will, bounds, comes on end,
Forgets school dooing, being therein train'd,
And of kind mannage, pig-like he whines
At the sharp Rowell, which he frets at rather
Than any jot obeyes; Seeks all foul means
Of boystrous and rough Jad'rie, to dis-seat
His Lord, that kept it bravely: When nought serv'd,
When neither Curb would crack, girth break, nor diff'ring plunges
Dis-root his Rider whence he grew, but that
He kept him 'tween his legs, on his hind hoofs on end he stands
That Arcites legs being higher than his head
Seem'd with strange art to hang: His victors wreath
Even then fell off his head: And presently
Backward the jade comes o'er, and his full poyze
Becomes the Riders load: Yet is he living,
But such a vessell 'tis that floats but for
The surge that next approaches: He much desires
To have some speech with you: Loe he appears.

[Enter **THESEUS, HIPPOLITA, EMILIA, ARCITE**, in a chair.

PALAMON
O miserable end of our alliance
The gods are mightie Arcite, if thy heart,
Thy worthie, manly heart be yet unbroken:
Give me thy last words, I'm Palamon,
One that yet loves thee dying.

ARCITE

Take Emilia
And with her, all the worlds joy: Reach thy hand,
Farewell: I have told my last hour; I was false,
Yet never treacherous: Forgive me Cosen:
One kiss from fair Emilia: 'Tis done:
Take her: I die.

PALAMON
Thy brave soul seek Elizium.

EMILIA
I'll close thine eyes, Prince; Blessed souls be with thee
Thou art a right good man, and while I live,
This day I give to tears.

PALAMON
And I to honor.

THESEUS
In this place first you fought: Even very here
I sundred you, acknowledg to the gods
Our thanks that you are living:
His part is play'd, and though it were too short
He did it well: your day is length'ned, and
The blissfull dew of heaven do's arowze you:
The powerfull Venus, well hath grac'd her Altar,
And given you your love: Our Master Mars,
Hast vouch'd his Oracle, and to Arcite, gave
The grace of the Contention: So the Deities
Have shew'd due justice: Bear this hence.

PALAMON
O Cosen,
That we should things desire, which doe cost us
The loss of our desire; That nought could buy
Dear love, but loss of dear love.

THESEUS
Never Fortune
Did play a subtler Game: The conquer'd triumphs,
The victor has the Loss: yet in the passage,
The gods have been most equall: Palamon,
Your kinsman hath confest the right o'th' Lady
Did lye in you, for you first saw her, and
Even then proclaim'd your fancie: He restor'd her
As your stolen Jewell, and desir'd your spirit
To send him hence forgiven; The gods my justice
Take from my hand, and they themselves become

The Executioners: Lead your Lady off;
And call your Lovers from the stage of death,
Whom I adopt my Friends. A day or two
Let us look sadly, and give grace unto
The Funerall of Arcite, in whose end
The visages of Bridegroomes we'll put on
And smile with Palamon; For whom an hour,
But one hour since, I was as dearly sorry,
As glad of Arcite: And am now as glad,
As for him sorry. O you heavenly Charmers,
What things you make of us? For what we lack
We laugh, for what we have, are sorry still,
Are children in some kind. Let us be thankfull
For that which is, and with you leave dispute
That are above our question: Let's goe off,
And bear us like the time.

[Flourish. Exeunt.

EPILOGUE

I would now aske ye how ye like the Play,
But as it is with School Boys, cannot say,
I 'm cruell fearefull: pray yet stay a while,
And let me look upon ye: No man smile?
Then it goes hard I see; He that has
Lov'd a young hansome wench then, show his face:
'Tis strange if none be here, and if he will
Against his Conscience let him hiss and kill
Our Market: 'Tis in vain, I see to stay ye,
Have at the worst can come, then; Now what say ye?
And yet mistake me not: I am not bold
We have no such cause. If th' tale we have told
(For 'tis no other) any way content ye
(For to that honest purpose it was ment ye)
We have our end; And ye shall have ere long
I dare say many a better, to prolong
Your old loves to us: We, and all our might,
Rest at your service, Gentlemen, good night.

[Flourish.

John Fletcher – A Short Biography

John Fletcher was born in December, 1579 in Rye, Sussex. He was baptised on December 20th.

As can be imagined details of much of his life and career have not survived and, accordingly, only a very brief indication of his life and works can be given.

His father, Richard Fletcher, was a successful and rather ambitious cleric. From being the Dean of Peterborough he moved on to become the Bishop of Bristol, Bishop of Worcester and finally, shortly before his death, the Bishop of London. He was also the chaplain to Queen Elizabeth.

When he was Dean of Peterborough, Richard Fletcher, witnessed the execution of Mary, Queen of Scots. It was said he "knelt down on the scaffold steps and started to pray out loud and at length, in a prolonged and rhetorical style, as though determined to force his way into the pages of history". He cried out at her death, "So perish all the Queen's enemies!" All very dramatic but the family did have strong links to the Arts.

Young Fletcher appears at the very young age of eleven to have entered Corpus Christi College at Cambridge University in 1591. There are no records that he ever took a degree but there is some small evidence that he was being prepared for a career in the church.

However what is clear is that this was soon abandoned as he joined the stream of people who would leave University and decamp to the more bohemian life of commercial theatre in London.

Unfortunately his father fell out with Queen Elizabeth but appears to have been on his way to rehabilitation before his death in 1596. At his death he was, however, mired in debt.

The upbringing of the now teenage Fletcher and his seven siblings now passed to his paternal uncle, the poet and minor official Giles Fletcher. Giles, who had the patronage of the Earl of Essex may have been a liability rather than an advantage to the young Fletcher. With Essex involved in the failed rebellion against Elizabeth Giles was also tainted by association.

By 1606 John Fletcher appears to have equipped himself with the talents to become a playwright. Initially this appears to have been for the Children of the Queen's Revels, then performing at the Blackfriars Theatre.

Commendatory verses by Richard Brome in the Beaumont and Fletcher 1647 folio place Fletcher in the company of Ben Jonson, although it is not known when this friendship began. Jonson, of course, was a leviathan of English Literature, so admired that many of his literary friends and colleagues were simply known as 'Sons of Ben'. Fletcher's frequent early collaborator, Francis Beaumont, was also a friend of Jonson's.

Fletcher's early career was marked by one significant failure; The Faithful Shepherdess, his adaptation of Giovanni Battista Guarini's Il Pastor Fido, which was performed by the Blackfriars Children in 1608. In the preface to the printed edition of his play, Fletcher explained the failure as due to his audience's faulty expectations. They expected a pastoral tragicomedy to feature dances, comedy, and murder, with the shepherds presented in conventional stereotypes – as Fletcher put it, wearing "gray cloaks, with curtailed dogs in strings." Fletcher's preface is however best known for its pithy definition of tragicomedy: "A tragicomedy is not so called in respect of mirth and killing, but in respect it wants [i.e., lacks] deaths, which is enough to make it no tragedy; yet brings some near it, which is enough to make it no comedy." A comedy, he went on to say, must be "a representation of familiar people." His preface is critical of drama that features characters whose action violates nature.

In that case, Fletcher appears to have been developing a new style faster than audiences could comprehend. By 1609, however, he had found his stride. With Beaumont, he wrote Philaster, which became a hit for the King's Men and began a profitable association between Fletcher and that company. Philaster appears also to have begun a trend for tragicomedy. Fletcher's influence has also been said to have inspired some features of Shakespeare's late romances, and certainly his influence on the tragicomic work of other playwrights is even more marked.

By the middle of the 1610s, Fletcher's plays had achieved a popularity that rivalled Shakespeare's and cemented the pre-eminence of the King's Men in Jacobean London. After Beaumont's retirement, necessitated by ill-health, and then his early death in 1616, Fletcher continued working, both singly and in collaboration, until his death in 1625. By that time, he had produced, or had been credited with, close to fifty plays. This body of work remained a major part of the King's Men's repertory until the closing of the theatres in 1642 due to the Civil War.

At the beginning of his career Fletcher's most important collaborator was Francis Beaumont. The two wrote together for close to a decade, first for the Children of the Queen's Revels, and then for the King's Men. According to an anecdote transmitted or invented by John Aubrey, they also lived together in Bankside, sharing clothes and having "one wench in the house between them." This domestic arrangement, if it existed, was ended by Beaumont's marriage in 1613, and their dramatic partnership ended after Beaumont fell ill, probably of a stroke, that same year.

At this point Fletcher had written many plays with Beaumont and several others on his own. He seems to have been regarded as quite a talent although it should be remembered that playwrights were required to be prolific, to easily work with other collaborators and to produce work of quality and commercial appeal very quickly.

The King's Men, run by Philip Henslowe, was the most prestigious of the theatre companies and Fletcher now had an increasingly close association with it.

Fletcher collaborated with Shakespeare on Henry VIII, The Two Noble Kinsmen, and the now lost Cardenio, which some scholars say was the basis for Lewis Theobald's play Double Falsehood. (Theobald is regarded as one of the best Shakespearean editors. Whether his play is based on Cardenio or on some other is not absolutely known although Theobald certainly promoted it as his revision of the lost Shakespeare/Fletcher play.)

A play that Fletcher also wrote by himself at this time, The Woman's Prize or the Tamer Tamed, is also regarded as a sequel to The Taming of the Shrew.

In 1616, with the death of Shakespeare, Fletcher now appears to have entered into an enhanced arrangement with the King's Men on very similar terms to Shakespeare's. Fletcher would now write exclusively for the King's Men until his own death almost a decade later.

As well as continuing his solo productions Fletcher was still collaborating with other playwrights, mainly Philip Massinger, who, in turn, would succeed him as the in-house playwright for the King's Men.

Fletcher's popularity continued throughout his life; indeed during the winter of 1621, he had three of his plays performed at court. His mastery is most notable in two dramatic types; tragicomedy and the comedy of manners.

John Fletcher died in 1625, it is thought of bubonic plague which, at the time, was undergoing further outbreaks.

He seems to have been buried in what is now Southwark Cathedral, although a precise location is not known. There is much made of an anecdote that Fletcher and Massinger (who died in 1640) share the same grave but it is more likely that both are buried within a few yards of each other and that the stone markers in the floor have confused the issue. One is marked 'Edmond Shakespeare 1607' and the other 'John Fletcher 1625' refers to Shakespeare's younger brother and the playwright. The churchyards were, more often than not, completely over-crowded and breeding grounds for disease. Precise record keeping was not a practiced skill.

During the later Commonwealth, many of the playwright's best-known scenes were kept alive as drolls. These were brief performances, usually condensed into one or two scenes and with the addition of music or song to satisfy the taste for plays while the theatres were closed under the Puritans. At the re-opening of the theatres in 1660, the plays in the Fletcher canon, in original form or revised, were by far the most common productions on the English stage. The most frequently revived plays suggest the developing taste for comedies of manners. Among the tragedies, The Maid's Tragedy and, especially, Rollo Duke of Normandy held the stage. Four tragicomedies (A King and No King, The Humorous Lieutenant, Philaster, and The Island Princess) were popular, perhaps in part for their similarity to and foreshadowing of heroic drama. Four comedies (Rule a Wife And Have a Wife, The Chances, Beggars' Bush, and especially The Scornful Lady) were also stage mainstays.

Despite his popularity, and it appears he was held in higher regard than Shakespeare at this time, his works steadily lost ground to those of Shakespeare and to new productions from other playwrights.

Since then Fletcher has increasingly become a subject only for occasional revivals and for specialists. Fletcher and his collaborators have been the subject of important bibliographic and critical studies, but the plays have been revived only infrequently.

Due to the frequent collaborations between all manner of playwrights, and the revisions carried out in later years, having a settled list of authorship to any given set of plays can be problematic. The works of Fletcher and others of this period most definitely fall into this category. It is as well to take into account that during this period theatres were quite often closed either due to outbreaks of the plague or to the prevailing political and moral climate. Printers, anxious to provide materials that would sell, were not above changing a name or two to enhance sales.

Although Fletcher collaborated most often with Beaumont and Massinger, it is believed that Massinger revised many of the plays some time after their original production. Other collaborators including Nathan Field, William Shakespeare, William Rowley and others also can be seen distinctly in Fletchers' works. Many modern scholars point out that Fletcher had many particular mannerisms but other playwrights would also duplicate these at times so allocating exact contributions of anyone to a play is somewhat of a detective case in many instances. However from the original folio printings or licensing via the Master of the Revels (the statutory licensing authority to approve and censor plays as well a hand in publication and printing of theatrical materials) as well as contemporary notes a fairly precise bibliography of the works can be given with only a few plays lacking substantial authority and provenance.

John Fletcher – A Concise Bibliography

This bibliography gives the most likely date of writing together with when published, revised or licensed by the Master or the Revels (This position within the royal household was originally for royal festivities, ie revels, and later to oversee stage censorship, until this function was transferred to the Lord Chamberlain in 1624).

Solo Plays
The Faithful Shepherdess, pastoral (written 1608–9; printed 1609)
The Tragedy of Valentinian, tragedy (1610–14; 1647)
Monsieur Thomas, comedy (c. 1610–16; 1639)
The Woman's Prize, or The Tamer Tamed, comedy (c. 1611; 1647)
Bonduca, tragedy (1611–14; 1647)
The Chances, comedy (c. 1613–25; 1647)
Wit Without Money, comedy (c. 1614; 1639)
The Mad Lover, tragicomedy (acted 5 January 1617; 1647)
The Loyal Subject, tragicomedy (licensed 16 November 1618; revised 1633; 1647)
The Humorous Lieutenant, tragicomedy (c. 1619; 1647)
Women Pleased, tragicomedy (c. 1619–23; 1647)
The Island Princess, tragicomedy (c. 1620; 1647)
The Wild Goose Chase, comedy (c. 1621; 1652)
The Pilgrim, comedy (c. 1621; 1647)
A Wife for a Month, tragicomedy (licensed 27 May 1624; 1647)
Rule a Wife and Have a Wife, comedy (licensed 19 October 1624; 1640)

Collaborations

With Francis Beaumont
The Woman Hater, comedy (1606; 1607)
Cupid's Revenge, tragedy (c. 1607–12; 1615)
Philaster, or Love Lies a-Bleeding, tragicomedy (c. 1609; 1620)
The Maid's Tragedy, Tragedy (c. 1609; 1619)
A King and No King, tragicomedy (1611; 1619)
The Captain, comedy (c. 1609–12; 1647)
The Scornful Lady, comedy (c. 1613; 1616)
Love's Pilgrimage, tragicomedy (c. 1615–16; 1647)
The Noble Gentleman, comedy (c. 1613; licensed 3 February 1626; 1647)

With Francis Beaumont & Philip Massinger
Thierry & Theodoret, tragedy (c. 1607; 1621)
The Coxcomb, comedy (c. 1608–10; 1647)
Beggars' Bush, comedy (c. 1612–13; revised 1622; 1647)

Love's Cure, comedy (c. 1612–13; revised 1625; 1647)

With Philip Massinger
Sir John van Olden Barnavelt, tragedy (August 1619; MS)
The Little French Lawyer, comedy (c. 1619–23; 1647)
A Very Woman, tragicomedy (c. 1619–22; licensed 6 June 1634; 1655)
The Custom of the Country, comedy (c. 1619–23; 1647)
The Double Marriage, tragedy (c. 1619–23; 1647)
The False One, history (c. 1619–23; 1647)
The Prophetess, tragicomedy (licensed 14 May 1622; 1647)
The Sea Voyage, comedy (licensed 22 June 1622; 1647)
The Spanish Curate, comedy (licensed 24 October 1622; 1647)
The Lovers' Progress or The Wandering Lovers, tragicomedy (licensed 6 December 1623; rev 1634; 1647)
The Elder Brother, comedy (c. 1625; 1637)

With Philip Massinger & Nathan Field
The Honest Man's Fortune, tragicomedy (1613; 1647)
The Queen of Corinth, tragicomedy (c. 1616–18; 1647)
The Knight of Malta, tragicomedy (c. 1619; 1647)

With William Shakespeare
Henry VIII, history (c. 1613; 1623)
The Two Noble Kinsmen, tragicomedy (c. 1613; 1634)
Cardenio, tragicomedy (c. 1613)

With Thomas Middleton & William Rowley
Wit at Several Weapons, comedy (c. 1610–20; 1647)

With William Rowley
The Maid in the Mill (licensed 29 August 1623; 1647).

With Nathan Field
Four Plays, or Moral Representations, in One, morality (c. 1608–13; 1647)

With Philip Massinger, Ben Jonson and George Chapman
Rollo Duke of Normandy, or The Bloody Brother, tragedy (c. 1617; revised 1627–30; 1639)

With James Shirley
The Night Walker, or The Little Thief, comedy (c. 1611; 1640)
The Coronation c. 1635

Uncertain
The Nice Valour, or The Passionate Madman, comedy (c. 1615–25; 1647)
The Laws of Candy, tragicomedy (c. 1619–23; 1647)
The Fair Maid of the Inn, comedy (licensed 22 January 1626; 1647)
The Faithful Friends, tragicomedy (registered 29 June 1660; MS.)

The Nice Valour is possibly by Fletcher revised by Thomas Middleton;

The Fair Maid of the Inn is perhaps a play by Massinger, John Ford, and John Webster, either with or without Fletcher's involvement.

The Laws of Candy has been variously attributed to Fletcher and to John Ford.

The Night-Walker was a Fletcher original, with additions by Shirley for a 1639 production.

Even now there is not absolute certainty on several of the plays. The first Beaumont & Fletcher folio of 1647 contained 35 plays and the second folio of 1679 added a further 18. In total 53 plays.

The first folio included The Masque of the Inner Temple and Gray's Inn (1613), and the second The Knight of the Burning Pestle (1607), widely considered Beaumont's solo works, although the latter was in early editions attributed to both writers. Fletcher himself said that Beaumont was attributed so-authorship of many works that belonged solely to Fletcher or to other collaborators.

One play in the canon, Sir John Van Olden Barnavelt, existed in manuscript and was not published till 1883.

William Shakespeare – A Short Biography

The life of William Shakespeare, arguably the most significant figure in the Western literary canon, is relatively unknown. Even the exact date of his birth is uncertain. April 23rd, the date now generally accepted to be the date of his birth, is a result of a scholarly mistake and the appealing coincidence of its being also the day of his death.

That so little is known about a writer with such great literary scope and accomplishment has naturally invited speculation and conspiracy theories about the authenticity of his authorship, his influence and even his existence.

Shakespeare was born in Stratford-upon-Avon in 1565, possibly on the 23rd April, St. George's Day, and baptised there on 26th April. His father was John Shakespeare, a successful glover and alderman who hailed from Snitterfield. His mother was Mary Arden, whose father was an affluent landowner. In total their union bore eight children; William was the third of these and the eldest surviving son.

Although there is no hard evidence on his education it is widely agreed among scholars that William attended the King's New School in Stratford which was chartered as a free school in 1553. This school was only a quarter of a mile from the house in which he spent his childhood, but since there are no attendance records existing it is assumed, rather than known, this was the base for his education.

Although the quality of education in a grammar school at that time varied wildly the curriculum did not, a key aspect of which, by royal decree, was Latin, and it is undoubtable that the school will have delivered an intensive education in Latin grammar, drawing heavily on the work of the classical Latin authors. If Shakespeare did attend this school then it is very likely the starting point for the fascination with and extensive knowledge of the classical Latin authors which would inform and inspire so much of his work began.

Little more detail is known of William's childhood, or his early teenage years, until, at the age of 18, he married Anne Hathaway, who was 26 and from the nearby village of Shottery. Her father was a yeoman farmer, and their family home a small farmhouse in the village. In his will he left her £6 13s 4d, six pounds, thirteen shillings and fourpence, to be paid on her wedding day. On November 27th, 1582 the consistory court of the Diocese of Worcester issued a marriage licence, and on the 28th two of Hathaway's neighbours, Fulk Sandells and John Richardson, posted bonds which guaranteed that there were no lawful claims to impede the marriage along with a surety of £40 to act as a financial guarantee for the wedding.

The marriage was conducted in some haste since, unusually, the marriage banns were read only once instead of the more normal three times, a decision which would have been taken by the Worcester chancellor. This haste is no doubt due to the child Anne delivered their first child, Susanna, six months later. Susanna, was baptised on May 26th, 1583. Several scholars have voiced their opinion that the wedding was imposed on a reluctant Shakespeare by Hathaway's outraged parents, although, again, there is nothing to formally support the theory. It has been further argued that the circumstances surrounding the wedding, particularly those of the neighbourly assurances, indicate that Shakespeare was involved with two women at the time of his marriage. According to the theory proposed by the early twentieth century scholar Frank Harris, Shakespeare had already chosen to marry a woman named Anne Whateley. It was only once this proposed union became known that Hathaway's outraged family forced him to marry their daughter. Harris goes on to surmise that Shakespeare considered the affair entrapment, and that this led to his wholesale despising of her, a "loathing for his wife [which] was measureless" and which ultimately caused him to leave Stratford and her and make for the theatre. But equally other scholars such as John Aubrey have responded to this with evidence that Shakespeare returned to Stratford every year which, if true, would rather diminish Harris's claim that Hathaway had poisoned Stratford for Shakespeare.

Harris's theory aside, Shakespeare and Hathaway had two more children, twins Hamnet and Judith, baptised on February 2nd,1585. Hamnet, Shakespeare's only son, died during one of the frequent outbreaks of bubonic plague and was buried on the August 11th, 1596, at the age of only eleven.

Little is known of Shakespeare's life during the years following the birth of the twins until he appears mentioned in relation to the London theatres in 1592, apart from a fleeting mention in the complaints bill of a legal case which came before the Queen's Bench court at Westminster, dated Michaelmas Term 1588 and October 9th, 1589. Despite this period of time being referred to in scholarly circles as Shakespeare's "lost years", there are several stories, apocryphal in nature, which are attributed to Shakespeare. For example, there is a legend in Stratford that he fled the town in order to avoid prosecution for poaching deer on the estate of Thomas Lucy, a local squire. It is also supposed that Shakespeare went so far as to take revenge on Lucy, a politician whose Protestantism opposed Shakespeare's Catholic childhood, by writing the following lampooning ballad about him:

> A parliament member, a justice of peace,
> At home a poor scarecrow, at London an ass,
> If lousy is Lucy as some folks miscall it
> Then Lucy is lousy whatever befall it.

However amusing the ballad and legend may be in imagining the life of a young Shakespeare, youthfully mischievous and still developing the wit, sense of adventure and humour which would become integral aspects of his writing, there is simply no evidence either to support the theory or to suggest that Shakespeare penned the ballad. Alongside this are suggestions that he began his theatrical career while minding the horses of the patrons of the London theatres and that he spent some time as a schoolmaster employed by one Alexander Hoghton, a Catholic landowner in Lancashire, in whose will is named "William Shakeshafte". However, this was a popular name in the Lancashire area at that time and there is no evidence that this referred to Shakespeare. The wealth of his writing makes it a frustrating exercise to learn more of his life and the manner in which he achieved those outstanding and lionized works.

Interestingly, the reference to Shakespeare in 1592 which ends the "lost years" is a piece of theatrical criticism by playwright Robert Greene in *Groats-Worth of Wit*. In a scathing passage Greene writes "...there is an upstart Crow, beautified with our feathers, that with his *Tiger's heart wrapped in a Player's hide*, supposes he is as well able to bombast out a blank verse as the best of you: and being an absolute *Johannes factotum*, is in his own conceit the only Shake-scene in a country." From this entry we can make some important inferences which shed light on Shakespeare's career, the first of which is that to be acknowledged, even negatively, by a playwright such as Robert Greene, by this point he must have been making significant impact on the London stage as a writer. Also of significance is the very meaning of the words themselves, for it is generally acknowledged that Shakespeare is being accused of writing with a lofty ambition beyond his capabilities and, more importantly, the capabilities of his contemporaries who were educated at Oxford and Cambridge. Within this remark, then, is an inherent snobbery which Shakespeare would come to resent and ultimately challenge in his writing. Though Greene's parody of "Oh, tiger's heart wrapped in a woman's hide" makes reference to *Henry VI, Part 3*, it is likely that Greene's opinion of Shakespeare was in part informed by another of Shakespeare's plays which was heavily criticised, *Titus Adronicus*, believed to have been written between 1588 and 1593. It was his first attempt at tragedy, almost prototypical, and was written at a time when, according to the scholar Jonathan Bate, he was "experimenting with ways of writing about and representing rape and seduction". Drawing heavily on the sixth book of Ovid's *Metamorphoses* as its main source of inspiration for the rape and mutilation of Lavinia, it offended the sensibilities of the more highbrow members of its audience, whilst presumably also simultaneously intimidating them with its detailed knowledge of Ovid, a writer typically considered the reserve of the university-educated. Not only, then, was Shakespeare demonstrating a knowledge of classical literature which they thought befitted only a traditional scholar and thereby shining a light to the snobbery and exclusivity of such an education, but he was doing it radically and brilliantly.

By 1594 the Lord Chamberlain's Men had recognised his worthiness as a playwright and were performing his works. With the advantage of Shakespeare's progressive writing they rapidly became London's leading company of players, affording him more exposure and, following the death of Queen Elizabeth in 1603, a royal patent by the new king, James I, at which point they changed their name to the King's Men.

Before this success, though, several company members had formed a partnership to build their own theatre which came to be on the south bank of the river Thames, the now-famous and reconstructed Globe theatre. Though it is unclear precisely what Shakespeare's involvement in this venture was, records of his property and investments indicate that he came to be rich during this period, buying the second-largest house in Stratford, called New Place, in 1597, which he made his family home. Prior to this he was living in the parish of St Helen's Bishopsgate, north of the River Thames. He continued to spend most of his time at work in London and from about 1598-1602, he seems to have lived in the Paris Gardens area of Bankside south of the river near The Globe.

Despite efforts to pirate his work, Shakespeare's name was by 1598 so well known that it had already become a selling point in its own right on title pages.

An interesting aside is that theatres were mostly constructed on the south bank of the Thames (then part of the county of Surrey) as performing in London itself was thought to be a bad influence on the masses and subject to periodic bouts of censorship, repression and closing of venues which in the City itself was mainly courtyards and open areas at the many Inns.

Excluded from the City purpose built theatres began to be constructed outside the City limits. This area of the Thames though was rough and naturally vibrant with all sorts of characters, many of them of dubious nature or even criminal. It was also prone, due to its over-crowding and bad sanitation, to bouts of bubonic plague and other diseases particularly during the summer which was a further reason for the theatres there being closed. The Curtain, The Rose, The Swan, The Fortune, The Blackfriars and of course The Globe were all purpose built and situated here, some with an audience capacity approaching 3,000.

The first known printed copies of Shakespeare's plays date from 1594 in quarto editions, though these quarto editions are often considered "bad", a term referring to the likelihood of specific quarto editions being based on, for example, a reconstruction of a play as it was witnessed, rather than Shakespeare's original manuscript. The best example of such memorial reconstruction can be found in the differences between the first and second quarto editions of *Hamlet*. In examining Hamlet's most famous soliloquy, "to be or not to be", we can immediately recognise significant differences. First, the familiar second quarto version:

> To be, or not to be; that is the question:
> Whether 'tis nobler in the mind to suffer
> The slings and arrows of outrageous fortune,
> Or to take arms against a sea of troubles,
> And, by opposing, end them.

And, by contrast, the first quarto version:

> To be, or not to be, I there's the point,
> To Die, to sleep, is that all? I all:

For scholar Henry David Gray the first quarto lines are emblematic of "a distorted version of the completed drama filled out and revised by an inferior poet" and based, he goes on to argue, on the fractured memories of the play as witnessed and performed by the actor playing Marcellus. Gray, and several other critics, consider the first quarto a pirated copy, printed in haste without the writer's permission in an attempt to make quick money following the success of the play in the theatre. In understanding the significance of Marcellus to the theory it is imperative to note that the authenticity of each quarto is based on its similarities to the version of the play found in the first folio, printed in 1623 and believed to be authorised by Shakespeare. Therefore, since in the folio version of *Hamlet* the "to be or not to be" soliloquy is virtually identical to that of the second quarto, it is believed that the second was authored by Shakespeare himself and that the first, by its considerable differences, must therefore be in some way compromised. However, when read in comparison to the folio version, the only character whose lines are almost entirely perfect are those spoken by Marcellus, which, since dramatic practice at the time was for actors to be given only their own lines and three or four word 'cues' based on the lines preceding theirs, suggests that the first quarto is a memorial reconstruction of the play written by the actor who played Marcellus. Having committed his own lines to memory he was able to reproduce them accurately, but was left to fill in the remaining lines and plot from memory which accounts for the truncated and often vastly inferior writing in the first quarto.

According to the remaining cast lists from the period, Shakespeare remained an actor throughout his career as a writer, and it is thought he continued to act after he retired his pen. In 1616 he is recorded in the cast list in Ben Jonson's collected *Works* in the plays *Man in His Humour* 1598) and *Sejanus His Fall* (1603), though some scholars consider his absence from the list of Jonson's *Volpone* evidence that, by 1605, his acting career was nearing its end. Despite this in the First Folio he is listed as one of "the Principle Actors in all these Plays", several of which were only staged after *Volpone*.

By 1604 he had moved again, remaining north of the river, to an area near St. Paul's Cathedral where he rented a fine room amongst fine houses from Christopher Mountjoy, a French hatmaker and Huguenot.

The Anglo-Welsh poet John Davies of Hereford wrote in 1610 that "good Will" tended to play "kingly" roles, suggesting he was still on stage, perhaps now performing the more mature kings such as Lear and Henry VI. There has even been the suggestion that Shakespeare played the ghost of Hamlet's father, though there is little evidence to suggest it.

In 1608 the King's Men purchased the Blackfriars theatre from Henry Evans, and according to Cuthbert Burbage, one of the most highly regarded actors of the time, "placed many players" there "which were Heminges, Condell, Shakespeare, etc." A 1609 lawsuit brought against John Addenbrooke in Stratford on the 7th of June describes Shakespeare as "generosus nuper in curia domini Jacobi" (a gentleman recently at the court of King James) which indicates that by this time he was spending more time in Stratford. A likely cause of this was the bubonic plague, frequent outbreaks of which demanded the equally frequent closing of places of public gathering, principle among which were the theatres. Between May 1603 and February 1610 the theatres were closed for a total of 60 months, meaning there was no acting work and nobody to perform new plays. Though in 1610 Shakespeare returned to Stratford and it is supposed lived with his wife, he made frequent visits to London between 1611-14, being called as a witness in the trial *Bellott v. Mountjoy*, a case addressing concerns about the marriage settlement of Mountjoy's daughter, Mary. In March 1613 he purchased a gatehouse in the former Blackfriars priory, and spent several weeks in the city with his son-in-law John Hall, a physician, married to his daughter Susanna, from November 1614.

No plays are attributed to Shakespeare after 1613, and the last few plays he wrote before this time were in collaboration with other writers, one of whom is likely to be John Fletcher who succeeded him as the house playwright for the King's Men.

In early 1616 his daughter Judith married Thomas Quiney, a vintner and tobacconist. He signed his last will and testament on March 25th, of the same year, and the following day Quiney was ordered to do public penance for having fathered an illegitimate child with a woman named Margaret Wheeler who had died during childbirth which had enabled Quiney to cover up the scandal. This public humiliation would have been embarrassing for Shakespeare and his family.

William Shakespeare died two months later on April 23rd, 1616, survived by his wife and two daughters.

According to his will the bulk of his considerable estate was left to his elder daughter Susanna, with the instruction that she pass it down intact to "the first son of her body". However, though Susanna and Judith had four children between them they all died without progeny, ending Shakespeare's direct lineage. Also in his will was the instruction that his "second best bed" be left to his wife Anne, likely an insult, though the bed was possibly matrimonial and therefore of significant sentimental value.

He was buried two days after his death in the chancel of the Holy Trinity Church in Stratford-Upon-Avon.

The epitaph on the slab which covers his grave includes the following passage,

> Good frend for Iesvs sake forbeare,
> To digg the dvst encloased heare.
> Bleste be ye man yt spares thes stones,
> And cvrst be he yt moves my bones

which, in modern translation, reads

> Good friend, for Jesus's sake forbear,
> To dig the dust enclosed here.
> Blessed be the man that spares these stones,
> And cursed be he that moves my bones.

At some point before 1623 there was a funerary monument erected in his memory on the north wall of Stratford-upon-Avon which features a half-effigy of him writing, and which likens him to Nestor, Socrates and Virgil.

On January 29th, 1741 a white marble memorial statue to him was erected in Poets' Corner in Westminster Abbey.

Though there have been many monuments built around the world in memory of Shakespeare, undoubtedly the greatest memorial of all is the body of work which became the foundation of Western literary canon and an inspiration for every generation.

William Shakespeare – A Concise Bibliography

1589	Comedy of Errors (Comedy)
1590	Henry VI, Part II (History)
	Henry VI, Part III (History)
1591	Henry VI, Part I (History)
1592	Richard III (History)
1593	Taming of the Shrew (Comedy)
	Titus Andronicus (Tragedy)

Venus and Adonis (Poem)

1594   Rape of Lucrece (Poem)
        Romeo and Juliet (Tragedy)
        Two Gentlemen of Verona (Comedy)
        Love's Labour's Lost (Comedy)

1595   Richard II (History)
        Midsummer Night's Dream (Comedy)

1596   King John (History)
        Merchant of Venice (Comedy)

1597   Henry IV, Part I (History)
        Henry IV, Part II (History)

1598   Passionate Pilgrim (Poem)
        Henry V (History)
        Much Ado about Nothing (Comedy)

1599   Twelfth Night (Comedy)
        As You Like It (Comedy)
        Julius Caesar (Tragedy)

1600   Hamlet (Tragedy)
        Merry Wives of Windsor (Comedy)

1601   Troilus and Cressida (Comedy)
1601   Phoenix and the Turtle (Poem))

1602   All's Well That Ends Well (Comedy)

1604   Othello (Tragedy)
        Measure for Measure

1605   King Lear (Tragedy)
        Macbeth (Tragedy)

1606   Antony and Cleopatra (Tragedy)

1607   Coriolanus (Tragedy)
        Timon of Athens (Tragedy)

1608   Pericles (Comedy)

1609   Cymbeline (Comedy)
        Lover's Complaint (Poem)

1610   Winter's Tale (Comedy)

1611   Tempest (Comedy)

1612   Henry VIII (History)

As regards his 154 sonnets it is almost impossible to date each individually though collectively they were first published in 1609, with two having been published in 1599.

Printed in Great Britain
by Amazon